H O W   T O   S A Y

GOODBYE

WORKING THROUGH PERSONAL GRIEF

JOANNE SMITH & JUDY BIGGS

Aglow Publications

A Ministry of Women's Aglow Fellowship, Int'l.
P.O. Box 1548
Lynnwood, WA 98046-1558
USA

Cover design by David Marty

Unless otherwise noted, all scripture quotations in this publication are from the Holy Bible, New International Version. Copyright 1973, 1978, 1984, International Bible Society. Other versions are abbreviated as follows: KJV (King James Version), TAB (The Amplified Bible).

ISBN 0-932305-82-2

Joanne: I lovingly dedicate this book
to my late husband, Duane,
who through his death
has taught me a great deal
about life.

Judy: To my precious husband, Steve,
who prayed,
prodded, and
praised me
all along the way.

To our core: Linda, Kathy, Karol, Barb, and Ed.
Our kids: Amy, Kevin, Jeanne, and Karissa.
Our prayer team: Michelle and Colette.

Acknowledgements

We are indebted to Gloria Chisholm and Aglow Publications for believing in us, and to the wonderful people of the Grief Release classes for sharing their pain, their stories, their love, and their willingness to get well.

Contents

Introduction

This is a how-to book. But unlike many how-to books, we are constructing an emotional project rather than building kitchen cabinets. We want to hand you the tools to rebuild a broken heart. Your loss may be death, divorce, disability, empty-nest syndrome, or even financial. Whatever the loss, the process is relatively the same.

Joanne understands loss from both ends of the spectrum. Besides losing her husband, father, and many other relationships, she is a skilled and caring counselor. She also is a member of the Bereavement Network, an association of professionals from hospitals, hospices, and other grief-related agencies in the Northwest. She is well-recognized as a grief counselor and receives referrals from medical doctors as well as national support groups such as Mothers Against Drunk Drivers (MADD) and Compassionate Friends. Joanne has produced her own video series, "Grief Release." She and her team of trained volunteers have taught the Grief Release program in as distant lands as Kenya, Africa.

I (Judy) have walked through multiple losses including close family members, personal trauma, my husband's broken neck, miscarriage, and major relocations. I have walked beside Joanne for the past ten years and shared her grief at an intimate level in addition to working professionally with her in leading Grief Release groups and providing music therapy from the piano. For the past eight years, I have worked as Associate Director of One to Another.

After spending more than four years leading Grief Release classes, we have helped many people work through loss. We sensed the need to write a simple manual, capturing both the essence of grief and the solution to releasing the intense pain.

Since grieving people are overwhelmed by lengthy reading material, we offer an easy format, understandable skills, and a bright promise of hope that *if* you decide to tough it out and work through the pain, you indeed *will* get well.

1

...

My Story/
Your Story

"Turn over, Duane, you're snoring."

Duane made an odd noise but no verbal response.

"Roll on your side, Honey."

Again nothing.

I climbed out of bed and headed for the light switch.

He forced a guttural wheeze, and I realized something was terribly wrong. Sudden panic seized me as my attempts to awaken him failed. The blue cast to his skin confirmed my fears.

I ran to the kitchen where our two phones hung side by side on the wall and dialed the emergency number. My body began to shake uncontrollably. "My husband has just had a heart attack. Please hurry!"

The man on the phone fired questions at me, keeping me on the line.

"Why aren't they here yet? Where are they?" I asked. His attempts to reassure me did nothing.

With the other phone, I dialed my neighbor. "Marilyn! Duane's not breathing. I think he's had a heart attack."

Marilyn and Dave arrived within the minute through the back door. The paramedic on the phone continued emergency instructions as Dave lifted Duane's body out of the waterbed for CPR. I relayed instructions to Marilyn, who stood down the hall. She tossed them to Dave in the bedroom.

"When will they be here?" I sobbed and prayed and trembled.

"They're here." Marilyn announced finally and ushered in two men with stretcher and lifeline paraphernalia.

Moments later at the hospital, when I saw the doctor's serious expression, I braced myself for the worst. "Mrs. Smith, your husband is dead." Amy, our eighteen-year-old daughter, crumpled into my arms. Marilyn and Dave stood nearby in shock.

"Dead." Until now no one had dared utter that ugly word. My husband was dead at age forty-six.

"I need to go in and see him," I said. I knew his spirit was with the Lord, but I wanted to hold him one last time and say goodbye.

The nurse led Amy and me into the emergency room. Through streams of tears, I told Duane how much I loved him, how he had been such a sensitive, supportive friend. How strong he was. What a good provider. What a good father. I kissed his face over and over. I took his hands and thanked him for how hard he had worked for us.

Amy watched and cried and followed my example. "You were such a good daddy. I loved you so much." Words of appreciation poured out of her aching heart.

The warmth of his body allowed us one last memory. A time of family closeness . . . a goodbye we would treasure and never forget.

As we turned to leave, I realized the nurse had witnessed our goodbyes. Tears welled up in her eyes as she said, "You must have really loved that man."

Dave, Marilyn, Amy, and I stood numbly at the emergency entrance as two more close friends arrived and hurried into our arms. "We lost him. He's with Jesus," I told them. We embraced and cried and held each other tightly. It was 5:00 a.m., the day before Easter. The longest day of my life.

Grief—if you're in it, you probably know it. Your details may differ, but your pain contains the same elements—unrelenting, gnawing anguish. Grief stabs at all our hearts at some time or another. Your grief may be caused by the death of a friend, child, marriage, relationship, or even an expectation. But grief is grief.

Because I have grieved, I understand the heartache of losing. No matter the cause of loss, we can make it through the process of grief. The process takes time and work. No one has instant answers or computerized formulas. We must forge through the pain and tough it out. Healing is possible.

Grief is the process of putting back together the pieces of a broken heart—a hole so deep in the middle of your heart that it aches and hurts and you think it will never stop.

Grief has three stages: shock, suffering, and release. The purpose of this book is not so much to define grief, but to help you embrace your grief and work through some tough but practical principles that will enable you to release your grief and get well.

Jesus was "acquainted with grief" and "has borne our griefs" (Isa. 53:3, 4 KJV), so we know he understands it. Our problem occurs because most of us are not acquainted (familiar, knowledgeable, versed) with grief and don't understand the process of working through it. We may be embarrassed by its seizure of our souls and frustrated by our inability to appropriate our faith to this devastating trauma.

Grief causes a major change in our emotions, life-style, and ability to relate to a non-grieving world. Whether your loss is the death of someone near and dear, a job, a dream, or a treasured expectation, the emotions emitting from grief will grip you at the least expected moments and threaten to bare your naked soul to the world.

Grief Release class members often share the helplessness of feeling overcome with grief while at work, shopping, or when triggered by sights and sounds associated with their loss. Sometimes the very uncomfortableness of those moments spur us into getting help.

You may wish to run from your pain. Sally tried that. Her husband committed suicide. For an entire year she ran. She traveled to different parts of the world, and upon returning she found she was only one year further away from her healing.

OBSTACLES THAT KEEP US FROM GRIEVING

Obstacles barring us from releasing our grief span from trying to mold our emotions around other's expectations to embarrassment over the nature of the loss.

Many people expect us to get well in a matter of weeks. If we would have had surgery, they would give us at least a month and possibly a year depending on the severity of our illness. But not with grief. People are uncomfortable around us, and they communicate either openly or behaviorally, "Hurry up and get well so I can be comfortable around you!"

If our loss has to do with AIDS or abortion or divorce, we may be so consumed with hiding the loss that we fail to embrace and tackle it.

In America, we are a fast-paced society. We eat instant breakfasts, quick and easy lunches, and microwave dinners. The carryover effect of our productivity-oriented values cause us to ram our hurts into a time-compactor, hoping we can achieve instant release from our pain. But alas, the pain of grief refuses to be disposed of without surfacing elsewhere. And so we become sick.

SICKNESS

Researchers comparing the health of grievers with non-grievers find mourners vulnerable to both illness and premature death. In 1944, Erich Lindemann discovered that mourners are at high risk levels for seven deadly diseases: heart attack, gastrointestinal tract cancer, high blood pressure, chronic itching and skin eruptions, rheumatoid arthritis, diabetes, and thyroid malfunction.[1] More recent studies in the British Medical Journal have confirmed Lindemann's work.

In a study of cardiac patients, Dr. James Lynch, author of *The Broken Heart,* found that mourners run two- to two-and-one-half times the normal risk for heart attack when compared to non-mourners, and depending on where they live, three- to three-and-one-half times the risk for gastrointestinal tract cancer.[2]

At a forum of the American Heart association, researchers disclosed that loneliness increases the risk of illness and premature death. People cut off from society—without spouses, friends, or community ties—have a death rate twice as high as those of the same age who are socially involved.[3]

Drs. Lisa F. Berkman and Lester Breslow, in *Health and Ways of Living*, revealed the results of a study of nearly five thousand men and women, ages thirty to sixty-nine, in Alameda County, California. They discovered that being married, staying in frequent touch with friends and relatives, and belonging to a church or other social group are important factors for maintaining health after significant loss.[4]

Janice Kiecolt-Glaser, Ph.D., associate professor of psychiatry at Ohio State University College of Medicine, says the stress of a marital breakup increases production of certain immunity-lowering hormones, making these people more prone to illness.[5]

According to Dr. Glen W. Davidson, as many as eighty-nine percent of the general public polled in 1980 understood mourning to be an illness, whose characteristics must be suppressed either by medicine, alcohol, or through sheer determination or exercise of faith.[6]

Four months after Duane died, I started a new job, complete with new opportunities, new relationships, and new challenges. I had difficulty embracing my new identity as Joanne Smith, a forty-five-year-old single.

The only way I knew how to cope was to throw myself into my job. I met hundreds of new people, organized meetings, trained Bible study leaders, led worship, taught a Bible study, counseled, and attended grief seminars in an attempt to close up the hole in my heart.

One evening while directing a meeting, I became ill and passed out. When I opened my eyes, several men circled me. I flushed with embarrassment and reassured them I was fine.

But "fine" evolved into a week of chest pains, landing

me in the intensive-care heart ward of the hospital. Two days after I was admitted, I was awakened early by the blaring hospital intercom. "Code ninety-nine, Code ninety-nine." People hurried in to the room next door. Code ninety-nine meant someone was near death. The rescue team tried to save the man, but he died. I glanced at the calendar date on my watch; it was October 21, six months to the day since Duane died. The total isolation I felt deepened. I knew that my heart had always been perfectly fine.

What am I doing in here? I asked myself.

The results of the tests were negative, but the doctor's harsh diagnosis cut me to the quick. "Mrs. Smith, nothing is clinically wrong with your heart. Your problem is that you're not handling your husband's death very well. You'd better get help."

If ever I felt like giving up, that was the day. I wondered if the pain would ever go away. Would I ever be normal and healthy again?

Well, I am. But not until making the decision to allow myself to grieve. I gave myself permission to cry and searched for a way to resolve my grief and cooperate with God in the healing of the horrible hole in my heart.

Some people try Bandaid cures like tranquilizers, hoping to put the lid down on grief. When it's time to throw away the pills, the pain remains, having not budged an inch.

RELOCATION

Our mobility as a society can prove detrimental to our emotional health if we fail to establish new relationships.

The transience of our culture can hamper the resolution of grief. When we move from city to city, we tend to make fewer and fewer close relationships to avoid having

17

to give up those friendships at the next move. We may think we have created a safety net when the opposite is true. A loss can occur at any moment, and we are left to grieve alone.

We view loss as an illness—distasteful, painful, and to be avoided—like leprosy or cancer. We are so disgusted by the negative in an upscale, upbeat society that the reality of facing the unpleasant disturbs us.

This perspective of loss has permeated even the medical field. Most health care professionals treat grieving as an illness, regardless of the fact that medical and other health care research over the past decade totally contradicts this assumption.

Helping professionals including pastors and educators have customarily understood mourning as normal in life when people lived in the country. They treated grief as a disease *only* after people moved to the city and began relocating for better job opportunities. But we continue to move, and we find ourselves suddenly experiencing loss with an inadequate support system.

OUR EMOTIONALLY BANKRUPT SOCIETY

In our achievement-oriented society, we see tears as weakness. We may not verbalize it, but our underlying belief system says, "Big boys don't cry" or "Crying is a sign of weakness" or "Get your act together and keep it that way." Expressing our pain and vulnerability through tears is simply not socially acceptable or respectable in jet age America. And yet, we're becoming dedicated advocates of establishing meaningful relationships, revealing "the real thing" as the Coke ad declares. Since our needs and our beliefs seem to conflict, we opt for our age-old worldview and stifle the tears as best we can.

Three weeks after Duane died, my daughter Amy and

I were driving home from church. Amy began to cry and asked me, "Mom, why doesn't anyone ask us over for Sunday dinner like they did when Dad was alive?"

"We have a dreaded disease called grief. They're afraid of us. They don't know what to say. If we cried, they'd feel uncomfortable, so they just ignore us."

"That's not right," she responded.

"I know."

And it isn't. When we don't fit into other's emotional comfort zones, we're doomed for alienation until some enlightened, compassionate soul reaches out.

UNDECLARED DECREES

The privacy often associated with a divorce decree hinders us from experiencing the necessary closure allowing us to grieve the loss of a marriage, an expectation, a happily-ever-after storybook dream.

If you are divorced, you may intellectually realize that the marriage is over while not at all letting go of it emotionally. Since there's no funeral or closure-oriented decisions such as burying a loved one, you may find it difficult to bury the marriage. Your friends are probably uncomfortable talking about your divorce because they do not know your needs.

We need closure if we want to get well, and closing an expectation is even more difficult when the person associated with that lost expectation still walks the earth. Custody battles, child support, and property feuds may unsettle the finality of the closure, but saying goodbye deals with the "relationship," not the person. More about this later. If you're divorced, you can discover a creative way of commemorating closure.

UNMENTIONABLES: SUICIDE, AIDS, ABORTION

Many people in my Grief Release classes have a difficult time finding an understanding, listening ear. Those suffering the loss of a loved one from suicide, AIDS, or abortion feel even more isolated. The stigma attached to these types of losses inhibits the formation of an adequate support system. It is important to find two or three people who are strong and encouraging enough to come under you and support you when walking through these devastating types of losses. You'll need someone who is shock-proof, tight-lipped, and trustworthy.

The anonymity of a support group is especially helpful for people walking through what they may consider "unmentionable" losses.

YOU

Perhaps the biggest obstacle in overcoming your grief is you. You make the final decision whether or not you'll get well. You will have to forge through the pain, develop your grief-releasing skills, and allow yourself the time, effort, and vulnerability releasing grief requires. You will need to prepare a place in your schedule for an emotional shelter to release your grief. Will you do it? If so, read on.

2

...

Becoming Real: from 'Fraidy Cat to Velveteen Rabbit

The first step in getting well is becoming real. The classic children's story by Margery Williams, *The Velveteen Rabbit*, offers some practical insight into becoming real.

"What is REAL?" asked the Rabbit one day, when they were lying side by side near the nursery fender, before Nana came to tidy the room. "Does it mean having things that buzz inside you and a stick-out handle?"

"Real isn't how you are made," said the Skin Horse. "It's a thing that happens to you. When a child loves you for a long, long time, not just to play with, but REALLY loves you, then you become Real."

21

"Does it hurt?" asked the Rabbit.

"Sometimes," said the Skin Horse, for he was always truthful. "When you are Real you don't mind being hurt."

"Does it happen all at once, like being wound up," he asked, "or bit by bit?"

"It doesn't happen all at once," said the Skin Horse. "You become. It takes a long time. That's why it doesn't often happen to people who break easily, or have sharp edges, or who have to be carefully kept. Generally, by the time you are Real, most of your hair has been loved off, and your eyes drop out and you get loose in the joints and very shabby. But these things don't matter at all, be-·cause once you are Real you can't be ugly, except to people who don't understand."[1]

The first person I need to become real with is myself. If I don't recognize that I need help, I am stalemated at the onset.

How *do* we become real? By letting down our guard. Peeling away the mask. You spend your nights sobbing in your pillow but during the day you keep it carefully hidden. Decide to stop laughing on the outside and crying on the inside. Stop communicating that you're all right when you are not. That's protective dishonesty.

Dr. Larry Crabb calls people who work through problems this way shallow copers. Shallow copers deal with what they can handle, ignoring the rest. In contrast to shallow copers, troubled reflectors wrestle honestly with at least some of the disturbing parts of their lives for which they have no answers. Dr. Crabb states that shallow copers become troubled reflectors when something traumatic happens to upset their confidence in their ability to handle life, like a spouse leaving the family. They search for some way to cope without looking honestly at the issues in their own hearts and at the quality of their relationships.[2]

The grief process requires the integrity to admit, "I *am* hurting. The pain is excruciating. I don't know if I'm going to make it."

I've discovered in five years of teaching Grief Release classes that the people who have the most difficulty getting well are the ones the Skin Horse talks about. They

• break easily: wear their feelings on their sleeve, are overly sensitive and fearful that if they begin to cry, they will never stop;

• have sharp edges: know all the answers, are cutting with their anger but refuse to deal with the grief behind it;

• have to be carefully kept: preserve personal dignity at any price, even at the expense of getting well.

People who wear their feelings on their sleeves struggle with becoming real. If you fit into this category, you probably weren't real *before* the loss. You may be so sensitively aware of what people are thinking about you that you simply freeze at the thought of drawing your feelings to the surface.

Perhaps you believe that because the pain is so intense, your friends would turn off if they really knew what was going on inside of you. You may be thinking, "If I expose my pain to you, you won't believe me, love me, receive me, or help me." Those who break easily are afraid to unwrap the bandage binding their broken heart. They are too well-acquainted with feeling "out of control" emotionally and lack the skills and confidence to again face a flood of hopeless sobs.

Sharp-edged people are game players. Do you have a quick answer for your inner turmoil, but find yourself falling apart when you're alone? Are you unwilling to talk about your pain? Do you seethe with anger when you feel misunderstood, abandoned, and rejected? Under a thin veneer of appearing "okay" lies a core of anger and rage rooted in hurt. You may choose self-defeating ways of revealing your need to others, further undermining your healing process.

As Christian women in grief, we often don't want anyone to know our emotional vulnerabilities. We feel that spiritually we should have everything "together." Some believe that to be the Proverbs 31 woman of strength and dignity, we must watch our confession carefully. We aren't willing to let people know how markedly the loss has affected us. We resist ripping off our mask of cheerfulness, admitting honestly, "I am really having a tough time working through this loss. I need some help." The "dignity or die disorder" refuses others access to our tears. God forbid that anyone should hear our "irregular" heartbeat.

I had a strong belief in God long before Duane died. After he died, all I could do was sit in church and cry. Living by myself and climbing into an empty bed every night was hell on earth. I hated it. People expected me to continue to be Jovial Joanne. It was the pits.

If you've been the strong one, a model or mentor for others, you may find becoming real especially difficult. If you can draw on your previous strength, do so. It takes *more* courage to open up and reveal your hurt during loss. I'm sure you've discovered why. People respond differently to you when you're weak. They want to walk next to strong people. They're not thrilled to associate with someone who's vulnerable, confused, and unhappy. So, dropping our dignity involves a risk with a reward. We're now able to take a peek at our feelings.

We don't usually want to cry around our families because they depend on our strength. Some families grow weary of the constant crying accompanying early grief.

But as we choose to openly share our feelings with our family, we usually find a positive response. We will have initiated a new and needed camaraderie and openness in our family.

As I became real, the character of my life changed. Areas of my identity I formerly thought needed to be sacredly preserved didn't. A part of who I am deep inside began to emerge with a new softness and depth of the character of Christ. I stopped picking up a script to act the part of the "woman of faith" according to Joanne. My new-found vulnerability released me towards healing.

Dishonest clichés Christian people verbalize to their potential support system go something like this: "God is my total source. I don't need anything or anybody." "I'm trusting God for my every need." "When it gets dark I just praise the Lord." They hide behind these statements and shut down love and encouragement from others by their facade of faith.

Even the person strongest in the faith can't expect to walk through grief without some help. In 1 Corinthians 12:21 we read, "The eye cannot say to the hand, 'I don't need you!' and the head cannot say to the feet, 'I don't need you!' "

God *does* take care of us, but sometimes we need someone with skin on to say, "You can talk to me and be real."

We are created to be interdependent. This doesn't mean opening up and baring our soul indiscriminately, but being willing to share in a safe environment where people understand or at least sincerely want to help. In our pain, we often choose to alienate ourselves. Decide to risk becoming real. Reach out for help. Join a support group. What have you got to lose?

Being real is the S.O.S. of healing in releasing grief.

The first "S" stands for Sharing (feelings, confusion, failure, frustrations, fears—whatever emotions are trapped inside of you). The "O" is for Openness (honesty, vulnerability). The last "S" represents Sensitivity to your own needs.

Feelings are real. Becoming real happens when we learn how to express those feelings for the purpose of getting our hearts healed. It is okay to have feelings. They are neither right nor wrong. What's important is to understand them, embrace them, release what needs to be freed, and get well.

A major change is happening to you. Most of us are not equipped to walk through major changes without help. We may cry out for help in subtle ways only to be ignored.

I'm sure you're familiar with the 1967 stress study performed and published by Thomas B. Holmes and Richard Rahe.[3] They formulated a stress rating scale listing various life-change factors affecting our ability to cope. The list rates death of a spouse, divorce, and marital separation as the top three stressors.

If you've suffered a loss and you're numb, you're probably still in the shock phase. Reality has not yet set in. The shock phase forms a protective film over your emotions. At first this is desirable, but if you suspect you are denying the reality of your loss and its effect on you, use this checklist to see if your body is telling on you. Are you experiencing any of the following?

- disbelief
- confusion
- lack of concentration
- emptiness
- fear
- feeling deprived

- anger
- memory lapse
- loneliness
- hallucinations
- guilt
- the "if only's"

- crying spells
- insomnia
- sighing
- shaking
- lump in the throat
- withdrawing from people
- waves of grief

- nightmares
- restlessness
- sore muscles
- pressure in the chest
- constant talking about the person

This is a fairly complete list of the reactions to loss. You certainly won't experience all of them, but if you are in early grief, you will recognize your share of symptoms.

So you've read the list and realize you have some work to do. Most people can relate to one or more of the following unhealthy coping mechanisms of handling grief.

- Illness: ailments, symptoms, and sympathy
- Lethargy: checking-out
- Promiscuity: fill my empty arms
- Busyness syndrome: run till you drop
- Worrying: fear running wild

We've already discussed the tendency toward illness during the bereavement period in Chapter 1. If we know we're easy prey for illness and do nothing to prevent it, we fall sick by neglect. Failing to take necessary health precautions can get you stuck in the sickness phase.

Since we think physical illness is socially acceptable, we need not fear criticism from coworkers for taking sick leave. Sickness then becomes an unhealthy coping mechanism. Whether your ailments are consciously or involuntarily rooted, they are a second-rate substitute for really getting well.

Lethargy is another typical reaction to grief. You're so fatigued by depression that you go to bed, pull the covers over your head, and attempt to sleep away the pain. But when you awaken, the pain is still there. Your nightmare is *not* over, and you don't want to go on.

Scientists at the University of Michigan "agreed that social isolation alone is a 'major risk factor' for mortality, perhaps as much as that of cigarette smoking."[4]

Psychologist Sandra Levy at the Pittsburgh Cancer Institute "found that a factor called 'joy'—meaning mental resilience and vigor—was the second strongest predictor of survival time for a group of patients with recurrent breast cancer (first was the length of 'disease-free intervals')."[5]

David captures the agony of grief in Psalm 6:2-4, 6, "Be merciful to me, Lord, for I am faint; O Lord, heal me, for my bones are in agony. My soul is in anguish. How long, O Lord, how long? Turn, O Lord, and deliver me; save me because of your unfailing love. I am worn out from groaning; all night long I flood my bed with weeping and drench my couch with tears."

Promiscuity is a common reaction to grief, especially if the loss involved a mate. This is true even for those with normally high moral standards. When they lose their spouse, the devastation of loneliness ignites them into promiscuous relationships. The need for physical contact severs their moral fiber. Their grief only intensifies, further complicated by both guilt and now two unresolved relationships.

Kim, newly divorced from a long-term abusive marriage, fell into promiscuity while trying to work through the remnants of her life. In making a career change, she signed up for classes to catch up on the twenty-year gap filled by the now displaced homemaker. While in school, Kim met a distinguished, sensitive bachelor who cared about her pain. Or so she thought. Kim's compounded grief set her back almost a year.

The most prevalent response to grief is busyness. If we

can just keep our calendars full, we won't have time to think about the loss. And if we don't think about the loss, it will go away. So we sign up for everything under the sun, making appointments to meet for breakfast, lunch, dinner, and shopping, burying ourselves in our calendar, hoping to dull the pain in our heart.

Eventually, we're so worn out from all our running, we collapse in a heap. All the grief we stuffed or ignored surfaces. Finally, we realize we have a problem.

The final coping method to grief is worrying. Our problems loom like giants in a bonsai garden. We try to keep a positive attitude, but half our brain wars with the other half. We say to ourselves, "I can walk through this thing and come out okay." The opposing side shouts, "I'm never going to get well." The two sides volley, playing havoc with any semblance of emotional or mental stability we thought we had.

Worry means to divide the mind. "Yes, I can." "No, I can't." "Yes, I can." "No, I can't." Scripture tells us that a divided house cannot stand. "Any kingdom that is divided against itself is being brought to desolation *and* laid waste, and no city *or* house divided against itself will last or continue to stand" (Matt. 12:25 TAB). So it is with a divided mind.

So what is the answer? How do we move from the dysfunctional coping mechanisms above to a therapeutic road of release?

RECOGNIZE YOUR COPING MECHANISMS

What keeps you from becoming real about your grief? Is there anyone you can trust enough to share your pain? Are you willing to admit (emotionally, not merely intellectually) you have a problem?

One of the first steps is to identify your feelings, taking

an intangible mass of black sky, and separating it into single clouds.

For example, today I may feel depressed. I don't know why I'm having this particular reaction on this particular day at this particular time, but I'm in the depths of the pit.

Was it something someone said?

Was it triggered by seeing someone share an activity I can no longer share with my loved one?

Is it a special occasion (my lost loved one's birthday, a holiday)?

Have I been sleeping enough?

Am I eating nutritious meals?

Am I physically weak?

Becoming real involves asking hard questions. And answering them. Think through the past few days to see if a thread of re-occurring behaviors or situations have been triggering your depression, anger, or guilt. Then . . . talk about it. Unload your pain on some strong compassionate soul. Talking about your loss is the first step in becoming real and getting well.

Sometimes the layers of denial are so deep we can't seem to sort. Try getting your cues from what makes you cry or by glancing through the How Do You Feel Today chart on page 71. If you suffer from grief-induced insomnia, you're apt to be a little rummy anyway.

I suggest doing a loss history early in your grief to ascertain whether your current loss is the root of your grief or if you have prior unresolved losses. How did you deal with loss as a child? Did you stuff it, ignore it, or talk about it? Was your family open when discussing death or divorce? Did you attend funerals as a child? Did you say goodbye to pets or childhood friends who may have moved away?

Some people have difficulty becoming real because

they compare their loss to someone else's. They feel they don't have a right to grieve because they didn't lose a husband or child or one of the "big" losses. Grief is grief and no two people grieve alike. To punish yourself because you feel unworthy of grieving is the devil's lie to keep you depressed.

People who wear masks sooner or later have to remove them. Why not do it now and embark on the adventure of vulnerability? Ultimately, you'll be glad you did.

In the beginning, you may find it difficult to even be real with yourself. But as you gradually risk the loss of your dignity and some of your privacy, you'll discover new freedom in becoming that somewhat shabby but ever-loved Velveteen Rabbit.

3
...

Therapeutic Dialogue: Talk, Talk, Talk!

Talk! Talk! Talk! Talk! Talk! Talk! Talk! Talk! Talk! Talk!

Talking is the most obvious, least appreciated part of releasing grief. Even for non-verbal people, repetitive verbal expression of all the sights, smells, sensitivities, and sounds surrounding your loss releases an enormous amount of inner pain—bit by bit.

When you consider the millions of minutes shared with someone special, it is virtually impossible to sort out all those moments and say goodbye to them without investing a considerable amount of time in the "savoring" process. Savoring involves poignantly, lovingly, sometimes angrily replaying those moments in time that will never return. Talking as a sorting and releasing tool is invaluable.

MEN VS. WOMEN IN TALKING ABOUT GRIEF

The whole area of talking is based on how women see themselves. Women are brought up to see themselves as bonded to or in relationship with others. For example, little girls often grow up relating to dolls. At an early age, their role is a mother, homemaker, or a bride. Until recent years, these have been standard roles affecting our self-image.

Men, on the other hand, are taught to be independent and self-sufficient. As a result, the effects of loss tend to be much more intense for women.

Wolfgang and Margaret Stroebe of the University of Tubingen, West Germany, found that not only did women have more friends than men, but women used those friends as supports. The pain of loss is often eased, Stroebe says, "by talking to other people—by opening yourself to others, telling them about your loss. Now, women seem to be better able to do this than men." The idea that silence is manly when it comes to grief prevents men from getting well.[1]

During our small group discussions in Grief Release, women jump right in and talk. Men will share, but they usually wait until all the women finish, and then, if I gently nudge them, they will open up. When they do begin to talk, their honesty and sincerity reveals their deep pain so tenderly as they talk about their loss.

Researcher Ruth O'Brien of the University of Rochester School of Nursing found that "Women continued to talk about their loss, and men preferred to avoid the subject." This is further substantiated by a study of researcher Robert DiGiulio of the College of St. Rose in Albany, New York. DiGiulio discovered that widowed women with a close friend to talk to adapt to their loss better than those who do not have such support. Since men withdraw and women reach out, men have fewer people to turn to.[2]

We have very few men in the Grief Release classes compared to the number of women. This is partly because widows outnumber widowers more than five to one. Widowers are terribly isolated because they have lost their sole confidants. "And so, in bereavement, they lose the one person to whom they could talk," says Stroebe.[3]

Psychologist Carol J. Barrett found that widowers were more likely to feel lonely and depressed than widows were, that men needed more help around the house, and that they were less willing to talk about the feelings associated with their loss.[4]

When suffering the loss of a child, husbands and wives don't talk to each other about their emotional condition. They each withdraw; they don't want to increase their pain by being misunderstood and rejected by their spouse. After miscarriage, infertility, stillborn births, and Sudden Infant Death Syndrome, a high percentage of marriages break up. Different reactions occur because men and women place opposite values on certain types of loss.

Some people contend that motherhood is a more central role for women than fatherhood is for men. If this is true, then loss of the "mothering" dream is more devastating to women.

When the loss of a child occurs, a couple needs to keep lines of communication open. Keep up the lovemaking. Tenderness strengthens the marriage bond.

Even though there are marked differences between the grieving patterns of men and women, *no two people grieve alike*. We must not compare our grieving process with anyone else or allow others to place a timeline on our recovery period.

PRODUCTIVE DIALOGUE

Now that we've discussed why we need to talk, how do we open up and get all those feelings out?

How do you begin to talk to somebody? What if you're in grief and lack communication skills? We've told you you need to get out your feelings, express your loss verbally, but you're in a quandary as just how to open your mouth and express anything meaningful. Try this:

1. *Take one part of the relationship and talk about it completely.* Ramble on and on about that unique specific quality, habit, or experience of your lost loved one and how it affected you. Suppose your grandma died. She always fussed over you and made you chocolate chip cookies. Talk about how those cookies tasted. Describe the cookie jar. Talk about how fast the cookies disappeared when you were at Grandma's. Talk about the way she mixed the ingredients. Talk about how she insisted on using only real butter and baking them only eight minutes. Talk about where you ate the cookies. Did you sit out on the lawn, take them to the park, set a formal tea on the dining room table, or stand in the kitchen wolfing them down? Talk about anything and everything that has to do with the fact that you and Grandma will never again share "cookie time."

2. *Schedule creative, productive talking.* Make an appointment to talk. Since talking is such an important part of getting well, place it high on your list of daily or at least weekly activities.

Amy and I used to write down various areas of our relationship with Duane (vacations, home-life, holidays, etc.) and put the topical categories in a jar. Each week we shared lunch and "remembered Dad." Amy pulled out one piece of paper—our topic for the day. We talked. She described in detail her memories of her dad on vacation—the tennis games, the practical jokes, the dinners, the bike rides, and anything those memories triggered. We laughed and we cried all the while working through the "savoring" process of the one we loved so dearly.

3. *Tell your story and talk about your pain as many times as you can.* You may feel like it will perpetuate the grief, but the reverse is true.

Sara was aware of her need to talk about her son. She went to a different shopping center every day and found some compassionate soul who was willing to listen to her story. She was able to release a lot of her grief.

Sara discovered that the more she talked about an issue, the fewer details she needed to relate and the less emotion she experienced. After several months of "mall talking," she experienced noticeable healing.

She was eventually able to talk about both the good *and* bad parts of the relationship. When she could finally talk about the hard spots, she realized she was getting well.

4. *When it seems like no one wants to listen, persevere.* Someone is willing to hear you out.

One day not long after Duane's death, I was sorting through my teaching charts, looking for a particular topic. I happened upon the chart I'd made for Duane's last birthday six months before. The chart read, "Happy Birthday, Duane. Here are forty-six reasons why we love you." At Duane's forty-sixth birthday party, his friends spoke out forty-six character qualities as I wrote them down—fun, loving, strong, honest, caring, good sport, good father, dependable, generous. . . .

Since I was now in a new job where nobody knew Duane, I wanted to take the chart to work and share him with my new colleagues. Off I went, chart in hand.

I entered the building with a coworker who said, "Hi, Joanne. How are you?"

"Well, as a matter of fact . . . ," I tried to respond, but he disappeared before I could even finish my sentence.

As I turned the corner to my office, I ran into my secretary.

"Good morning, Joanne. Great day, isn't it?" she asked.

"I'm sure it is, but could I talk to you a minute?" I fumbled with the sign as my briefcase started to slip.

She ignored my request and walked on, seemingly in another world.

I finally arrived at my office. Since I shared it with another woman, I walked into her cubicle. "Good morning," I said. "I found this chart about Duane this morning. Could I tell you about it?"

Her telephone rang. "Oh, I'm sorry, Joanne, but . . . not right now."

Not now meant not at all. I so needed to talk about Duane.

I walked out of the office and down the hall where I ran into another associate. I must have looked pretty discouraged by that time.

"Hi, Joanne. What's that you're carrying? Are you okay?" he inquired compassionately.

"Oh, Dennis, do you have a minute? I found this chart from Duane's birthday party last April, and I'd sure like you to meet him," I admitted.

"Sure. Come on into my office. Let's talk."

5. *If no one is available or your feelings are too private, talk into a tape recorder.*

Marilyn found she was wearing out her family in her need for endless grief monologue. Also, some delicate issues needed to be talked about without fear of betrayal.

She discovered that talking into a tape recorder afforded her the listening ear she needed. She benefited from both the anonymity and accessibility of this electronic listener. She was able to more completely release her grief because she could "tell all" and share unedited feelings, memories, and frustrations of her grief process.

6. *If you find it extremely difficult to sort and pinpoint your feelings, join a grief support group.* Sometimes listening to others tell their story helps you define your own grief. In a grief support group, feelings common in grief are revealed; it helps round out our perspective, giving us hope. We may think, *If Sam has walked through this horrible place and is getting well, maybe I can too* or *I didn't think anybody else felt like that. Maybe I'm not crazy.*

WITH WHOM DO I TALK?

Find some good listeners—people who are willing to walk out their commitment to you. You probably have people who say to you, "If there's anything I can do for you, just call me." Although it's difficult, call them. Tell them, "I need to cry. I need to talk."

Simply look for listening ears. Don't look for advice at this stage. You may need to educate your listening candidate. Tell this person, "I don't need your expert advice— just your ears." See Chapter 10: Developing a Support System.

OTHER "PEOPLE" WITH WHOM TO TALK

1. *Talk to a teddy bear.* For a soft touch and a no-flack response, try your trusty teddy bear. You don't have one? Splurge. He (or she) is great therapy.

2. *Talk to the dog (or the cat).* Who besides God gives such unconditional love and has no appointment to meet?

39

3. *Talk to yourself.* It's even okay to answer yourself. Sometimes we need to hear ourselves speak out loud to better think, sort, and process our feelings.

4. *Talk to a professional.* If you're stuck in a particular area of your grief and progress is overwhelmingly slow, consult a trained grief counselor. Often it only takes a few sessions to get you over the hurdles.

5. *Talk to God.* You may wonder why God is last. He's first, of course, but grieving people are often out of touch with God for a variety of understandable reasons. David was in grief in much of the Psalms. Oftentimes, reading the Psalms aloud helps you release fear, anger, and loneliness in practical ways. Read Psalm 42. "Why are you downcast, O my soul?" (v. 5).

WHEN TO TALK

1. *During difficult times of day.* For me the dinner hour was a crucial time. For some people, depression hits in the middle of the night. If your friends have really made the commitment to support you, call them and talk to them, describing the rough places of your grief

2. *When triggered by sights, smells, or conversations about the person.* Many divorced people need to talk right after having an unsettling conversation with their former mate. Custody suits, finances, or jealousy over being replaced by a younger woman are just a few "trigger times."

"Oh, the comfort—
The inexpressible comfort—
Of feeling safe with a person.
Having neither to weigh thoughts
Nor measure words,
But pouring them all right out
Just as they are,

40

Chaff and grain together.
Certain that a faithful hand
Will take and sift them;
Keep what is worth keeping
And with a breath of kindness
Blow the rest away."

Dinah Mulock Craik (1826-1887)

4
...

Celebrations: Holidays, Birthdays, Anniversaries, and Other Formerly Special Days

Celebrations take on a whole new meaning when we are walking through grief. We are either numb or so emotionally volatile that we doubt our sanity. What happens in our emotional center when a "Formerly Special Day" (FSD) occurs?

BIRTHDAYS

Let's talk about birthdays. Everybody has one (or had one). In our culture, birthdays are often a big deal. We chart not only our chronological progress by birthdays, but gauge our socialization skills by our age as well. From the day of our baby's actual birth to his first, tenth, sixteenth, and twenty-first birthdays, we enjoy the excuse to celebrate life and love, family and friendship. When we join loved ones in celebrating thirtieth, fortieth, fiftieth,

43

sixtieth, and up birthdays, we become more tightly knitted into relationship by celebration. Memory ties related to birthdays dig deep into our hearts. The very sources of joy when our husband, child, or dear friend were near now bring sorrow when turning the calendar to "their" date, their birthday.

Even if you're walking through divorce, your children will still remember and celebrate your ex's birthday. Inevitably, a flood of memories will rush in—both pleasant and awful. How will you walk through these FSD's?

Mary delivered twin boys at five and a half months. Both boys died within hours after their births. After their deaths, Mary delivered a healthy baby girl and two years later another healthy girl. Each year, Mary and her two daughters pack up a picnic, birthday cake, balloons, and photographs of the boys and set out for the cemetery. They talk about the babies, sing happy birthday to them, and, for a short time, enjoy being part of a larger family.

Meredith and Allison now understand that they had brothers, that their brothers lived only a short while, and that they now live in heaven. Each year they better understand how sad it was for their brothers to die. Mom assures them that they'll all meet again in heaven.

Joan's sixteen-year-old son was killed in a freak accident. On her son's seventeenth birthday (just weeks after his death), Joan baked a cake and took a couple of Carl's friends to the beach. She asked the teens to write letters about Carl, to express why they loved him and what they now miss in his absence. Joan chose a beach they had never visited before. She knew the day would be difficult enough and didn't want old memories of past vacations to compound the event.

WEDDING ANNIVERSARIES

Wedding anniversaries are another difficult FSD to hurdle because they are compounded by the "lost dream" syndrome. We place such importance on the longevity of marriage that when a spouse dies or leaves the marriage, our dream of a twenty-fifth or a fiftieth wedding anniversary dies, too.

Anniversaries bring to mind a flood of memories spanning much of our lives and centered around the word *couple*. Walking past anniversary cards in the store compound the pain as well as watching our happy friends celebrate or our ungrateful ones complain about puny flaws in their mates.

Choose a good friend and tell him/her that you'd like to go out to dinner together to help get you through what would have been your anniversary. Explain that you might not be terrific company but that you only need love and support.

"FINALITY DAY" ANNIVERSARIES

The day your loved one died or left you or the day of your final divorce decree are "finality" days. These days trigger a sadness that you can best combat by again planning a new event to help bridge the past and the present and to remember what you had.

On the first anniversary of Duane's death, I organized a potluck of primarily new friends from my new church family. Since most of the people didn't know Duane, I supplied pictures, talked about him, and asked Amy to talk about him. After dinner, I asked the men to lay hands on Amy and pray for her. As she felt the touch of men's hands on her shoulders, she began to cry. She was so grateful for the opportunity to both share about her dad

45

and to bask in the warmth, love, and prayer from fatherly friends.

GETTING THROUGH THE HOLIDAYS

Holiday time! The whole world seems consumed with tinsel and glitter—but if you're grieving, you only feel the terrible hole in your heart. To counter the intense pain of the holiday season, here are some helpful thoughts shared by other bereaved people.

Please realize that grieving people have definite limitations. We do not function at normal capacity. We need to re-evaluate our priorities and decide what is really meaningful for us and our families.

Ask yourself these questions:

• What can I handle comfortably?

• Do I want to talk about my lost loved one at holiday celebrations?

• Can I handle the responsibility of the family dinner and/or holiday parties or do I need for someone else to take over some of these traditional tasks?

• Will I·stay home for the holidays or "run away" to a totally different holiday environment this year?

• Have I involved or considered my children in holiday planning?

• Do I really enjoy doing this? Do other family members really enjoy this?

• Is this a task that can be shared by other family members?

• Would Christmas be Christmas without doing this (baking Christmas cookies, sending cards, other traditions)?

• How many stockings shall we hang? Put them all up? Hang no stockings at all?

When it comes to Christmas stockings, try writing

thoughts and feelings about your loved one on notes and insert them in that special stocking. Family members are free to read them thus providing a special opportunity for younger children to express their feelings.

When seated around the holiday table, it is hard not to remember all those loved ones who once were part of the celebration and who are now no longer with us. Look closely into the faces of your family. See them for who and what they are, not what you would have them become to suit your own personal needs. It is not as though you can, or even should, forget about the past. Rather, try to fit it into the present in productive ways.[1]

Don't be afraid to make changes. Changes *can* make things less painful. You might want to:

• Open presents Christmas Eve instead of Christmas morning.

• Eat dinner at a different time.

• Attend a different church for your Christmas Eve service.

• Let the children take over decorating the tree, baking cookies, etc.

Your greatest comfort may come in doing something for others. Some people feel they can acknowledge their loss more meaningfully by:

• Giving a gift in memory of their loved one.

• Donating the money they would have spent on the loved one for a gift to a particular charity.

• Adopting a needy family for the holidays.

• Inviting a guest (foreign student or senior citizen) to share holiday festivities.

One family burns a "Special Candle" on all their Special Days to quietly include their "absent" loved one.

Christmas shopping is definitely easier if you make the entire list out ahead of time. Then, when one of those

"Good Days" comes along, you can get your shopping done quickly and with less confusion—the earlier the better.

If the thought of sending holiday letters is too exhausting, yet you discover that some of your friends are still unaware of your loss, try this: enclose the simple funeral service card inside the already bought greeting card. Others have found the response from friends is most rewarding.

Remember:

1. *Take one day at a time.* Today is all we have. "As your days, so shall your strength be" (Deut. 33:25). Yesterday is gone, tomorrow is not here, but we have today. Use it to the fullest.

2. *Be realistic.* Recognize we need to set limits by accomplishing the projects most meaningful for you and your family.

3. *Keep a record of your Thanksgiving and Christmas activities.* Add on or enhance—growth and change go hand in hand.

4. *Remember that when the "Special Day" arrives, it is not going to be as bad as you anticipated.*

5. *Keep photo albums as a reminder of the joyful times.* Keep on taking pictures in the new places.

6. *During the holiday season, give the gift of space.* Allow for periods of private, alone time within the structure of family togetherness. Let older kids watch TV by themselves. Parents may want to go out to the movies or to a restaurant or sleep in a bit later than usual.[2]

The first Christmas after Duane died, I decided I wanted to include him in our Christmas holiday. I asked each family member to come prepared to share one special gift that Duane had made or given them a previous

Christmas. My brother-in-law adamantly balked at the idea.

"That's a dumb idea, Joanne! I'm not going to do it."

"Well, that's what we're going to do this year, John. See you on Christmas." I gulped as I insisted on this plan to cope with Christmas.

Duane was creative with his hands and had often made handcrafted presents. I was sure this would help us all get through Christmas dinner.

Christmas came. After dinner we shared, laughed, and cried about the crazy and wonderful gifts Duane had so carefully given.

John came up to me after dinner. "This was a great idea. I'm sorry I gave you such a bad time about it," he admitted sheepishly.

NINE TIPS TO LIGHTEN YOUR HOLIDAY LOAD

1. *Make daily lists.* Get a calendar to see the whole picture. Think about last year. What would you like to repeat? What do you want to change? Mark your calendar for baking, cards, shopping, parties, etc. Make both a monthly and daily list. Follow it one task at a time.

   a. *Make your list in the morning or the night before.*

   b. *List your responsibilities in consecutive order.*

If you start writing cards, finish the job. If you decide to make cookie dough, go ahead and make the cookies before you fold clothes, vacuum, make phone calls, etc. Otherwise, you will be left at the end of the day with many unfinished tasks. Forget big cleaning jobs until next year. Make a list of "mini-jobs" for windfall moments—spare time that suddenly appears. Make a list of jobs to do while on the phone.

2. *Enlist help—delegate or stagnate.* One of our biggest mistakes is we think we have to do it all ourselves.

The belief that "to do it right I have to do it myself" is a motto we can clutch right up to a nervous breakdown.

3. *When possible, avoid or prevent interruptions.* Teach your children to respect your time. Let them have quiet time, so you can have some. Unplug the phone for thirty minutes. Some people define emergency as anytime they want to talk to you. Say, "I'm working on a project, and I can talk five minutes now, or I'll call you back at three o'clock. My door is closed, and I do not want to be disturbed."

4. *Always plan for the unplanned.* The unexpected usually happens. Traffic is heavy; meetings last longer; the project took three hours instead of two. You may be wrapping Christmas presents and run out of supplies. Prepare in order to avoid frustration or prepare to be frustrated. Allow at least an hour every day for unexpected interruptions.

5. *Plan efficiently.* Use the phone—let your fingers do the walking through the yellow pages. Consolidate trips. Mobility can be either an advantage or a curse. Mail early; shop off hours. Select one kind of gift and give it to several people. Use pretty boxes or have the gift wrapped.

6. *Keep things simple.* Make decisions not only on the basis of what looks good or seems good, but on how much of your time it will demand. When processing mail, handle each piece only once by practicing the four D's:

Do it now (pay the bill, answer the letter).

Delegate (pass it on for someone else to handle).

Delay it (put it in project file to deal with).

Dump it (into the trash can).

7. *Be punctual.* Promptness is the prince of politeness. You can avoid a great deal of stress by arriving places on time. Arriving late starts everything on the wrong foot. It shows poor planning and a low regard for the people or

event. It often leaves you irritable, embarrassed, and ready
to pick a family fight. Allow thirty minutes for unforeseen
delays. Get up and get going—mind over mattress.

8. *Match the task to your energy level.* If you are a
morning person, work on the projects requiring the most
energy in the morning. Grocery shopping will help keep
you moving in the afternoon.

9. *Be kind to yourself.* Feel blue about the holidays? If
the "poor me's" are getting to you, do something special
for yourself or someone more needy than you. Take a tea
break. Take a candlelight bubble bath. Read a chapter in a
book. Go for a walk. Buy a piece of your favorite candy—
indulge. Call a friend and tell her you need a muffin break.
Turn on the Christmas tree lights and enjoy.

CREATIVE IDEAS TO HELP SOMEONE IN GRIEF

One way to encourage a grieving friend during the
difficult holiday times is to organize the Twelve Days of
Christmas. Beginning with December 14th, plan and deliver one gift each day including Christmas Day. You will
need to know the best time to deliver each day without
involving the recipient. Call her office or ask close relatives or friends. Playing detective for a couple of weeks is
fun. The receiver will love the surprise of having a gift
waiting at a meeting or the hairdresser or your luncheon
date with her. The intrigue helps make the Christmas
season bearable.

Make each gift match up with the day of Christmas.
Here's what one friend did:

Day 1: one Christmas ornament
Day 2: a salt and pepper shaker
Day 3: three candles in a candleholder
Day 4: four placemats
Day 5: a five-dollar bill or a fifty-dollar bill

Day 6: six cinnamon rolls

Day 7: seven scriptures in a specially wrapped box

Day 8: an eight-pack of her favorite soda pop or juice

Day 9: nine bath cubes

Day 10: an appointment for a manicure

Day 11: eleven grocery items in a sack with a ribbon on it

Day 12: twelve beautiful long-stemmed roses delivered with a hug!

Another way to encourage your grieving friend is to adapt the Twelve Days of Christmas theme to the first anniversary of the day your friend's loved one died. Duane died the day before Easter, so my friend Mary took a large Easter basket, filled it with plastic eggs, and inserted something special inside each egg. I was to open one egg a day until the anniversary. Each egg held a small gift: lipstick, magnets, special paper clips, scripture verses, etc. On the anniversary day of his death, she delivered an Easter Lily with money in the egg. In a tangible way, she said, "I love you and want to show it."

A lot of thank you notes need to be written after a family member dies. One thoughtful friend bought me a whole roll of postage stamps. She also gave me a membership to the American Automobile Association (AAA), so that if I had a flat tire or car trouble, someone would be available to help.

A grieving person's energy level is greatly affected due to the emotional strain of loss. Offering physical help such as weeding the flower beds, cleaning bathrooms, painting, and wallpapering are all ways to support your friend.

Sending notes, calling during the most difficult time of the day (perhaps dinner time, or late at night or early in the morning), an invitation to lunch, and offering lots of hugs to help alleviate the "skin hunger" are all ways to walk another through grief.

Finally, after the initial hub-bub of flowers and cards have stopped, you'll realize that the hurting hasn't lessened at all. In fact, it is probably greater because the numbness is wearing off, and the realization of loss is painfully strong. *You* be the one to continue to care after most others have assumed the grieving is finished. Releasing grief takes a long time and your support could make all the difference!

Never ignore those Formerly Special Days. They won't go away because you ignore them. Establish new activities to help bridge the past with the present.

Even though life goes on, you don't need to walk through the holidays alone. No matter what, plan *something* to do—don't wait until the last minute. Make definite plans, however sketchy. Remember: this day is only twenty-four hours long. One day out of all of the days of the year. You're going to make it!

5
...

For Crying Out Loud: Giving Yourself Permission to Cry

A five-year-old once said, "My eyes are sad. I need to cry."

William Frey, biochemist and director of the Dry Eye and Tear Research Center in Minneapolis, says, "Emotional tears play a precise and central role in helping to restore the chemical balance of the body by excreting substances produced by the body in response to stress."[1]

Frey discovered that the lacrimal gland, which regulates tear secretion, concentrates and removes manganese from the body. The concentration of manganese, a mineral affecting mood alterations, is thirty times greater in tears than in blood serum. He also found that emotional tears have a different chemical makeup than irritant tears.[2]

Although women cry four times more often than men, they also have sixty percent higher prolactin levels.

Prolactin promotes tear production, which may explain the sex difference in emotional crying. Before puberty, boys and girls not only have similar prolactin levels, but similar crying frequencies.[3]

In a study at the University of Pittsburgh School of Nursing, psychiatric nurse Margaret Crepeau found that among 137 men and women, healthy people are more likely to cry and have a positive attitude toward tears than are those with ulcers and colitis, two conditions thought to be stress related.[4]

Further, Frey notes, children who suffer an inherited disease called familial dysautonomia have two things in common: They can't cry tears and they have an extremely low tolerance for emotionally stressful events.[5]

WAVES OF GRIEF

A wave of grief occurs when you start thinking about the person you lost. Feelings of depression, darkness, despair, loneliness, and hopelessness crash over you like an ocean wave. You think you're going to die and you wish you would. Take heart. It may last from ten minutes to two hours, but you will have accomplished much healing during that time. While the wave is breaking, don't stifle it. If you stuff that kind of pain, it goes down inside of you and ultimately causes anxiety attacks.

Let the wave of grief roll over you. Find a place to cry. If you're at work, go to the bathroom or walk around the building. If you're with other people, excuse yourself or ask permission to cry.

Healthy people are more likely to cry since emotional tears play a role in the ability to tolerate stress. Since eighty-five percent of the women and seventy-three percent of the men in Frey's surveys reported feeling better after crying, he suggested that we might feel physically and psychologically worse by suppressing our tears.[6]

Several months after Duane died, I chaperoned our church's teen choir at the Olympic games in Los Angeles. Both my fatigue and grief levels were high. We ministered fourteen hours a day, riding from site to site in a bumpy old school bus. One morning the youth director stood up on the bus and asked us all to turn to John 14. John 14 was Duane's favorite chapter in the whole Bible. As I began to read "in my Father's house are many mansions," I lost it. Sobs burst out of me as the kids stared and whispered among themselves.

"What's the matter with Joanne?" I heard one ask.

These kids knew Duane well as we had both worked with them for months on this Olympic project, memorizing Scripture and interacting with them. Since I thought they would understand, I stood and blubbered, "I'm having a wave of grief over Duane. This was his favorite Scripture. Would you give me permission to cry?"

They nodded their agreement, then gathered around and laid their hands on me. I continued to cry until the wave ebbed away. I had taken another step forward in the healing of my broken heart.

HEALTHY AND UNHEALTHY TEARS

Some people have little difficulty crying. In fact, they find it almost impossible not to cry. When they do, their tears seem to depress them even further.

There is a point in the crying process when the physical and emotional release has taken place, but we fail to move it to a point of hope. At the end of a crying session, we should feel better, not hopeless. If hopelessness shrouds itself around you, you can take several steps to get out. First, remember, grief is painful, but *you* decide if it will crush you or create new life in you.

Tears are beneficial as long as we learn to release them in a way that draws us to our God of hope. This is not meant to be a super-spiritual pat answer, but a workable truth. In Psalm 23:4 we read that we *will* encounter the "[deep, sunless] valley of the shadow of death." That valley affects all of us at some time or another in varying degrees. The entire verse in the Amplified Bible says, "Yes, though I walk through the [deep, sunless] valley of the shadow of death, I will fear or dread no evil; for You are with me; Your rod [to protect] and Your staff [to guide], they comfort me." When fear picks up where the tears left off, we've made a wrong turn.

In my early grief, I could not remember complete verses of Scripture, but I could encourage myself with fragmentary faith phrases like "I will fear or dread no evil," and "I'll never leave you or forsake you," and "God will finish the good work he started in me."

Every time a wave of grief hit, and I had ridden the wave to the sand with my tears, I chose mentally to encourage myself with those three truths. The pain was excruciating, but I could not allow fear and hopelessness to attach themselves to the pain. After years of pain and years of counseling, I knew where that road would take me.

Maybe you're not aware of the difference and where that line is. If you start to experience suicidal thoughts, you'll usually find them rooted in hopelessness and fear. Use your tears for healing, *then turn them* to hope little by little, bit by bit, until you can believe God does love you enough to get you through this tough time. He's done it plenty of times before.

I'm not afraid to cry. I'm not afraid to release the pain and be vulnerable in front of people, but I will not leave it there. Out of turmoil and suffering and total brokenness comes hope. It must. Although most people don't give you permission to express feelings, we need to anyway. We have to walk *through* the heartache, depression, and loneliness, but we can't stop there. Keep walking. We don't have to fear because HE IS WITH US. I cannot go on feelings. I have to go on knowings. The biblical truth is higher and stronger than heartache, suffering, and pain.

When the tears have subsided, say, "This is a dark place, God, but I don't have to fear evil or be afraid. My tears do not mean I choose to be afraid. I'll trust you in this dark place so that when I come through this, I'll be as pure as gold." If you stay in the morbid place, you begin to perpetuate the depression and the negative and devastation starts its insidious work. Sometimes I say, "Lord, this is the worst day of my life, but I'm going to keep walking. I may be lonely, but I'm not alone because you are with me." I turn it from the destructive to the healing because God's Word is truth even when I don't feel God's presence. It doesn't have anything to do with feelings. He said, "I'll never leave you or forsake you." Don't turn back to a negative tape.

Remember the Velveteen Rabbit in Chapter 1? When it comes to expressing tears, the rabbit would say something like this, "I need permission to cry. Stay by me. Hold my hand until I'm through it. Please reinforce the good qualities that you see in me. Pray for me; encourage me by affirming me. Give me some warm affectionate love. I need you."

Be like the little boy who said, "My eyes are sad. I need to cry."

6
...

Journaling: Write Your Heart Out

Journaling is one of the most effective healing tools in grief work. Journaling involves writing down your emotions on paper in a "Grief Journal." *Journaling is connected to journeying.* As you make your journey through grief, record your pain.

Do you have feelings like those in the following grief journal entries?

I feel so alone—separated from all the people around me. Why is my energy level so low? Why do I feel sometimes like I have nothing else to give—nothing left to restore what I have given out? Will life ever be back—no, I can't go back, but will life ever be full of joy, laughter, fun again?

61

How to Say Goodbye

I feel so bruised inside.

This has been a long week for me—each day has felt like a thousand years long. Sometimes I feel like I'm at a movie—watching life going on around me. I feel sad, rebellious, selfish, apathetic, lonely, frustrated, desperate, and exhausted.

Why am I so tired? I can hardly get out of bed and get moving! Is it because I am coming to the year mark of his death and don't want to face it? Is it because I know I have to keep going, and I really don't want to? I don't know what in the world the next step is. Help, help, help! Do I have the flu, and I just keep walking on? Everything inside me aches—my spirit, my soul, and my body.

A year has gone by—my life is one constant battle for survival.

My body trembles and shakes. My sleep is interrupted so much during the night. My daughter is without a job—no purpose—glued to the TV set. What is going on?

I feel like the odd man out most of the time. What is it I am feeling so deep inside me? What is going on? My heart is so heavy.

That cute little curly-headed baby at Burger King looked just like Mandy. I wanted to grab her and run. Why did Mandy have to die? I hurt so much. How will I ever get over this? I want my baby back.

My God, I am so shaky this morning. My heart aches, my whole body is falling apart.

I smelled her perfume today at the mall. I miss her so much.

Who left that yearbook by my bed? I had to look at it. If only I had helped him more. I feel like I failed as a mom. And now he's gone.

I saw him with that woman today. I hate him. And her—that home-wrecker. How could he do this to me after all these years? I miss him so much but he doesn't even care if I exist. Is this really happening to me? It's a nightmare.

WHAT IS JOURNALING?

Journaling is a(n):

1. *Outlet of expression.* This daily record of my emotional condition is a safety valve as on a hot water heater or pressure cooker, releasing a sense of balance in the midst of chaos and confusion.

2. *Analyzer.* It helps make sense out of what is happening to me. Journaling interprets emotions, crushing the boulders of fear in our carts into cotton balls. When you analyze on paper, your fears lessen because you see them in black and white. They no longer loom like giants over you. When you face them in written form unamplified by imagined what-ifs, they lose their power. I experienced so much fear regarding finances, my creativity was paralyzed. When I analyzed them on paper, peace came.

The fear in your grieving process may be about being alone, finances, social life, etc. Whatever the fear, writing and analyzing it readies you for the next step.

3. *Clarifier.* Writing clarifies and simplifies the myriad of questions prompted by loss. You will not get all the answers, but you can simplify the questions.

4. *Sorter.* In this culture, we are big on organization. During the grief process, all organization flies to the wind. If you would like some semblance of that part of your former life to return, try journaling. Journaling grants us a sorting process, allowing us to categorize our moods into anger, fear, rejection, loneliness, or whatever.

One woman reported violent feelings of anger at a coworker who ignored her loss. The coworker knew this woman well, was acquainted with her husband Bill, and yet ignored the loss verbally. She never talked about Bill or asked Sandy about her feelings of loss. One day at work, Sandy exploded.

"What's the matter with you? Didn't you even care about Bill? All you talk about is your plants and your car and your piddly little problems!" Sandy shouted as she stomped off.

Later, Sandy wrote about that conversation that caused such an irrational reaction. Journaling enabled her to sort out her feelings, understand them, and later make amends with her friend.

5. *Tuning tool.* When a piano is badly out of tune, it may take several tunings to bring it up to pitch. When we're in grief, our entire system is thrown out of tune. Each time we write about one specific part of our grief, we become more in tune with reality.

6. *Scrapbook or a file.* Just as a scrapbook is composed of bits and pieces of the activities of our lives, journaling is bits and pieces of our emotions. Simply write what you can whether it makes sense or not, and eventually all those scraps will outline the healing of your heart

from loss. Do not be concerned about how the pieces fit right now, only keep gathering the pieces.

7. *Heart monitor.* When you experience chronic chest pain, you usually go to a doctor. In grief, you experience chronic pain, but a doctor can't help much. What do you do? Do you ignore the pain because you can't document it on a medical chart? How about using your journal as an internal heart monitor? It will prove as effective as the medical one and costs only the price of a notebook and pen.

8. *Pacemaker.* We hear a lot about productivity. Exercise is a vital ingredient for increasing productivity. Reaching and maintaining your target heartbeat cadence is necessary for exercise to be effective. Just as pacing is important to physical strength, pacing ourselves emotionally through journaling is of even greater importance. Journaling slows us down to a pace where we can evaluate the true meaning of life.

9. *Memory jogger.* During the grief process, memory lapse is common. One way to combat poor recall is to keep a journal. I capture thoughts and feelings I would have otherwise forgotten. I may have intended to remember them, but in the grieving process, the brain is overloaded with stress and important thoughts disappear as quickly as they come. If I keep my journal handy at all times, I'm better able to record, release, or remember thoughts at will despite my temporary handicap of forgetfulness. I can fight the memory bandit because I'm ready for him.

10. *Track record.* After months or years of grief work, you may want to go back and follow your grief journey by rereading your track record. Journaling gives you a place to release your pain, while also providing you a permanent portfolio to track your growth.

11. *Twenty-four hour sounding board.* "I'm sorry, the doctor is out. His next available appointment is November 23, three weeks from Tuesday."

Have you ever heard those words? Availability is utmost in getting help through the grieving process. And it seems that when we hurt the most, help is least available. Most of the time we merely need someone to listen. Our journal becomes a twenty-four hour open switchboard to sanity. We ramble, rant, and often make no sense at all, but as we release those words on paper, we are getting well. Sounding off to our journal brings all the benefits of release and none of the guilt of interrupting someone's sleep.

12. *Time saver.* We often hear the slogan that it takes money to make money. So it is with time. It takes time to make time. If your responsibilities scream at you from early morn and your energy disappears before your list does, take heart. Journaling will save you hours in the counseling office, the doctor's office, as well as hours untangling the emotional damage caused by your unresolved grief in relating to your family and friends. It may seem at first like a time waster, but the opposite is true. Journaling is an addictive but productive habit. You won't want to stop even after your grief is resolved.

These tips won't do you a lot of good unless you pick up your pen and journal. A lot of people buy a journal but fail to write.

One hindrance is insecurity about writing ability. When I was a teenager, I won a work scholarship to a lovely camp in British Columbia. One day during mail call I received a letter from my deaf mother. I tore open the letter and began reading the latest news from home. While I was reading, the camp director called my name to come up front and participate in a skit. I placed my stack of mail on my chair and proceeded to the front. When the skit was over, I returned to my seat only to watch a group of guys reading and making fun of the letter from my mom.

"Who's this retard writing to you, Joanne?"

"Give me that!" I snarled. "That letter's from my mom and she's deaf. She doesn't write like you but she's not a retard!"

My macho friends were mortified and fell all over themselves apologizing. "Oh, Joanne, we're so sorry. We had no idea. Will you please forgive us?"

"Sure. But keep your hands off my mail."

My mom can't write in complete sentences. I understand her style of communication perfectly, and that's all that matters. So when it comes to writing, I have little sympathy for the students in my class who say they can't write. You will be the only one reading your journal. It doesn't matter if your sentences are fragmented, if you can't spell, or if your handwriting is illegible. It only matters that you write because writing down your feelings will help you get well.

So much of life does not make sense. We're full of confusion. Journaling helps release that confusion.

WHEN TO JOURNAL

I journal:

1. . . . *when I need to make sense out of my feelings.* What is happening to me? Why am I feeling so lonely and deprived?

One day as I drove to the mall, I stopped at a red light and casually glanced around. In the car next to me a couple hugged and kissed and affectionately expressed their love to one another. Depression fell like a sudden downpour. Drenched with despair, I could barely see out as the car behind me honked to notify me of the green light. As soon as I could, I turned around and drove directly home. I ran into the house, grabbed my journal, and furiously began to write. I wrote about not having someone to hold me and kiss me and tell me he loved me. I wrote about feeling deprived. I wrote about missing Duane so terribly. I filled up five or six pages in my journal. When I came to the end of my epic, I put down the pen and sighed aloud—one long, releasing sigh. I felt so much better that I grabbed my keys and proceeded to the mall. Journaling does help!

2. . . . *when I can no longer tolerate the pain.* Journaling is most effective when the pain is so intense that you literally can't stand it. You are finally at a place to express what is going on in your heart. Don't keep a diary of your daily activities but rather one of your moods, feelings of sadness, hopelessness, and deprivation.

3. . . . *late at night or early in the morning.* It's never too late at night or too early in the morning to journal. Your journal never gets tired.

HOW TO JOURNAL

Read the Emotion Barometer and Feelings Word List on pages 71-72. Circle one word that describes how you feel. Say, "I feel lonely today," "I feel abandoned," "I feel deserted," etc.

Ask yourself, "Why do I feel this way?" Then write what you feel. Whether it makes sense or not is unimportant.

Face your grief squarely and record your pain. Don't skirt touchy issues. Address your anger, your guilt, your jealousy, your "not nice" emotions. Feelings are feelings—they are neither right nor wrong. The pages of your journal will not talk back, they will not judge you, they accept you as you are. As you record your feelings, you will experience some release.

Because journaling may be a new discipline for you, ask someone to keep you accountable. Most grieving people don't write every day. It may be every other day or weekly or when the pain is most intense. Ask a friend to check up on your frequency and honesty in journaling. This person's job is not to read your journal, but just to make sure you're writing.

Keep in touch with your emotions. Learn to recognize when you are overreacting to people, when you become easily stressed, when your fatigue level is too high. Pay attention to your feelings so that you can better assess your emotional condition. Are you experiencing storms of anxiety, numbness, or any hints of relief?

Try to discover patterns in your grief and moods You may notice that you start to write in your journal at five o'clock every evening. You find you have a pattern of grief that occurs at dinner time because you only cook for one. Use your journal to get through that difficult time of day or night.

Sit down, take a deep breath, pick up your grief journal and your pen, and write. Evaluate the meaning of your life. Take time to slowly work through this process. Give yourself permission to record your journey one tear at a time. Recalling one memory will trigger another. WRITE—even if you don't know what to say!

PRINCIPLES FOR JOURNAL WRITING

• Be absolutely honest.

• A journal is private property—off limits to others for casual reading.

• A journal does not require great writing skill. I am

not writing for publication. I'm recording my thoughts and feelings for my own growth and release.

JOURNALING TESTIMONIALS

One woman discovered that there is a limit to the amount of internal pandemonium the human mind will tolerate. "When I reached my limit, my mind began dumping onto paper what it couldn't process internally," she said.[1]

"Journaling gives order to my thinking."

"Journaling helped remove the emotional clutter from my mind so I didn't continue to brood all day."

"I hate to write, and I really balked at the idea of journaling. In my mind, I imagined spending hours trying to look for the right words to describe my feelings. Writing a letter takes me an hour, so how could I have the energy and time to make that kind of commitment? One day I was so depressed that I actually sat down to write. The words flowed easily and quickly. I was amazed at how much better I felt. It really does work!"

Joanetta Hendel of *Bereavement Magazine* states that "the written expression of grief is unsurpassed in therapeutic potential."[2]

What more can I say? Journaling is one very important answer in walking through your grief to healing. What have you got to lose? Won't you try it?

How Do You Feel Today?

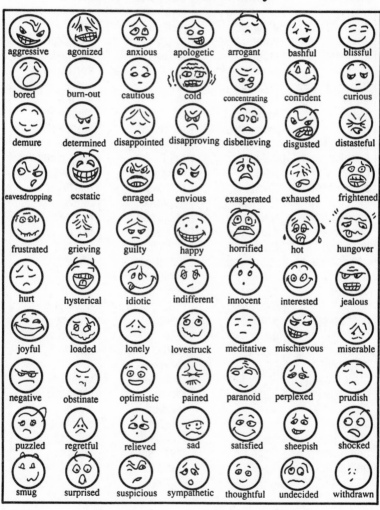

FEELINGS WORD LIST

active	down	infuriated	retortful
affected	drowsy	insulted	revengeful
alert	dubious	interested	scared
angry	easygoing	involved	shaky
annoyed	efficient	jealous	sick
anxious	embarrassed	jittery	skeptical
apathetic	empty	listless	sluggish
at ease	energetic	lost	sorrowful
bad-tempered	engaged	low	sorry
bitter	envious	mad	spiteful
bleak	excluded	malice	steaming
blue	exhausted	maligned	stopped
burdensome	explosive	melancholy	suffering
bushed	failure	mild	suspicious
calm	fatigued	miserable	sympathetic
clear-headed	fearful	morose	tearful
clutched up	forgetful	nervous	tense
concentrating	forlorn	obsessed	terrified
concerned	friendly	on edge	tired
confused	frustrated	optimistic	trapped
considerate	full of pep	out of it	tricked
deceitful	fuming	panicked	unable
deceived	furious	peeved	uncaring
defiant	gloomy	pessimistic	uncertain
depressed	grouchy	quiet	uneasy
destroyed	guilty	rage	unworthy
detached	happy	ready to fight	upset
discounted	hateful	rebellious	used
discouraged	heavy hearted	regretful	vigorous
disgusted	helpless	relaxed	vivacious
disgusting	hostile	relieved	weary
dismayed	hot	repulsed	weighed down
displeased	hurt	resentful	withdrawn
disregarded	hurtful	reserved	worn out
distressed	ignored	restless	worthless

7

...

Anger, Guilt, and Forgiveness: Bitter, Better, or "But Grrr . . ."

"I hate him, I hate him," the woman in the second row snapped.

"Tell me, why do you hate him?" I queried. Velma had hired a landscaper named Butch to trim her trees. While he was working, Velma's thirty-year-old daughter, Lucy, often visited her mom. Butch struck up a friendship with Lucy and began to visit her at her apartment several blocks away.

One night they had a terrible fight. Butch took the belt from Lucy's robe and strangled Lucy to death in her bed.

Velma hated Butch and understandably so. Butch murdered her daughter. "If only I hadn't hired him to work on my yard."

Anger consumed Velma during those early months.

Anger is a part of grieving. You feel angry because someone you loved has been taken away. That someone was important to you. Now that person is gone.

Anger surfaces in many forms, at unexpected times, and in a variety of intensities. Sometimes we are angry at everything and everyone. Anger is natural and normal in grief. Not everyone feels angry, but many people do. It's okay to feel angry. Remember, feelings are not right or wrong; they just are.

Anger can be caused by change. In the transitions of death or divorce, we feel alone and/or rejected. When unwanted change interrupts our lives, we feel invaded. This invasion leaves us vulnerable and thrown off balance. We lose our emotional equilibrium.

Just before Duane died, he loaned a man one thousand dollars on a gentleman's agreement without interest for about thirty days. The man had worked for Duane and was now going through a divorce.

Then Duane died. I discovered we had no mortgage insurance, a one-time two hundred dollar Social Security death benefit, and no life insurance. Since Duane was an independent contractor, I would receive no further income. He was building a home at the time of his death and I was in financial trouble. Amy was about to graduate from high school, and I didn't even have enough money to buy groceries for the family graduation party.

Two months had lapsed since Duane had loaned this man the money, so I called and asked him to return it. "Hi, Charlie. This is Joanne. Are things better for you?" I asked.

"I'm hanging in there," he responded.

"I just called to let you know I'm having a tough time financially. I wondered if you could return the thousand dollars that Duane loaned you."

"What thousand dollars?" he retorted. "You have no proof that Duane ever loaned me a thousand dollars. It's your word against mine. I don't owe you any money." He hung up.

Well, I was angry—I mean *livid* with rage. How could he do this to me? After all we had done to help him . . . .

When in grief, angry feelings may intensify. Your emotions are raw and if anger exists, it will surface. It needs to be extracted. If it isn't, it will express itself in destructive ways, including physical illness.

Listen to yourself and gauge your anger level. Are you overreacting? Do you say things you're sorry for later? Are your words cold and biting, leaving a bitter taste in your mouth? You may be seething with hostility. If you find yourself spewing angry words, you may face consequences in relationships that are beyond restoring.

Anger can only be extracted when recognized for what it is—pent-up energy. The following physical changes indicate the stress caused by anger, hurt, grief, and disgust:

Are your muscles tense around the eyes?

Is your jaw set and your teeth clenched?

Are your throat muscles tight?

Has your pulse rate accelerated?

Are your hands doubled up into fists or even slightly closed?

Do you feel any tension across the upper and lower back?

Is breathing becoming more rapid?

Is your stomach tense, knotted up, quivering, or upset?

Do your leg muscles feel taut?

We see two patterns here—a speeding up of the rhythm of our body (circulation and breathing) and a tightening up of the muscles. The body is making preparations to fight or take flight.

If you are experiencing these reactions, take that angry energy and do something constructive. We'll offer some suggestions later in this chapter.

HURT

To differentiate between anger and hurt is difficult. Many times when the root of our anger is hurt, we automatically seek revenge first, and express the anger second, and almost forget about the source of it all—the hurt. Remember Velma in the beginning of this chapter? Her foremost emotion blared out, "I want to get him!" Yet, the deep, underlying hurt and grief was really the root of her anger.

COMMUNICATION RULES FOR RESOLUTION

1. *Focus on one issue at a time.* Resolving a single issue is a challenge; resolving several at once is impossible.

2. *Deal with conflict before it reaches the boiling point.* Lucy in Peanuts says, "If I can't be right, I'll be wrong at the top of my lungs."

Losing our temper carries with it feelings of raw power and allows us to control the situation momentarily, but when we blow up we've lost control, not gained it. Usually, explosion discharges verbal blast—insults, accusations, profanity, etc.

3. *Open up and talk about it.*

    a. *Express your grievances, confusion, and pain.*

    b. *Remember that others can't read your mind.*

    c. *Silence is ambiguous.* "What is she thinking? Is she still angry?"

    d. *Don't exaggerate—overgeneralization blocks*

resolution. Don't say, "You never listen" or "You always make us late."

e. *No cheap shots.* The better two people know each other, the more ways they know to make each other wince with a cheap shot to a vulnerable spot. Strike at a woman's weak spot, and watch her defenses rise up, and the chances for resolution go down.

Human beings are both the toughest and most fragile things God put on earth. We need each other's protection not exploitation.[1]

Matthew 7:12 says, "Do to others what you would have them do to you."

WHAT DO WE DO WITH ANGER?

1. *Express it.* This is the quickest way to get rid of it. Learn how to release anger effectively.

One way to dissolve anger is to release it via a venting partner. A venting partner is someone you trust who will time you for three minutes while you blow off steam verbally. You can say anything you want because this person has committed to not process what you are saying but to simply provide ears on the other end of the telephone or a nonresponsive face at which you can direct your anger. If your anger is still raging after the first three minutes, your venting partner gives you an additional three minutes. Then, whether you're finished or not, you're done. Six minutes of explosive, unbridled, verbal rage is all you get. When the six minutes are over you simply say, "Thanks for your time. Goodbye." And hang up the phone. No advice, no guilt, no P.S.'s. Your steam has been vented, and you usually feel better without endangering anybody.

2. *Exercise.* Exercise is another way to use some of that pent-up energy caused by anger. Any activity

involving hitting or kicking a ball—tennis, racquetball, or volleyball all help.

You might want to pick up some old dishes at a garage sale to have on hand for anger release. Can't you see yourself smashing dishes? Maybe you could hurl them into a dumpster so you don't have to clean up the mess. You might end up laughing at yourself and never throw a dish, but that's a lot better than keeping your anger bottled up.

Some people pound on a pillow, a teddy bear, or a piano. Others squish rotten tomatos between their fingers.

3. *Journal.* Speed writing in your journal helps dissipate anger. Don't think, just write—the faster the better. Write about your feelings. Elaborate on all the irrational thought patterns, your fears, your hostility, that "stupid so and so" and whatever's racing through your mind. You can always tear it up after you're finished. The release of writing is what counts.

4. *Find a good counselor* and work it through in the counseling room. Some people are trained or gifted in drawing out your feelings so that you can better understand your anger.

Expressing your feelings allows you to focus on love, a healthier and more productive response. *Deal with your anger now.* Plan whatever action you need to take, but don't swallow up your anger. Admit it so healing can flow.

5. *Don't leave unfinished business.* Unresolved anger leads to bitterness. I remember several years back when Duane had loaned five thousand dollars to John, a man in our church who was starting a promising business. John was well-established and full of integrity. Duane's attorney drew up the necessary loan papers. The term of the

loan was set for ninety days.

After ninety days, John asked Duane for an additional ninety-day extension to the loan. Duane agreed. After the second ninety days, John began to avoid Duane like the plague. He refused Duane's phone calls and made himself scarce at church. Whenever Duane approached him, he slithered away.

Duane's normally easy-going, loving attitude began to change. He became sharp with me and Amy as cynicism invaded his personality. He became so angry that his anger turned to bitterness.

One day, I confronted him about how his attitude was affecting our family life. He admitted becoming bitter over the loan and said he would take care of it.

He picked up the phone and arranged a meeting with a third party—someone he knew had great influence with John. As we entered the mediator's office, John was seated at a table. Duane laid the contract on the table, then began tearing it to shreds.

"John, I believed in you and your business. I believed that you were a man of your word. I've called you, and you haven't returned my calls. I've tried to speak with you at church, but you've avoided me. I've done everything I can think of to resolve this thing, but you've thwarted my every attempt. I've allowed the stress over this broken contract to affect our friendship, my family, and my relationship with the Lord. Tonight, I want you to know that this contract is paid in full. If you ever make a million dollars, I don't want one penny of this returned. It's finished." Duane handed him the shredded papers.

John began to weep. The mediator began to cry. Duane stood to his feet, walked around the table, and laid his huge hands on John's shoulders and began to pray for him.

When Duane Smith put his hands on anyone, they were aware of his strength. (Duane's hands were so big that when we bought his wedding ring, the largest ring size was too small. The jeweler told us that the next size was a bracelet.)

After praying a loving prayer of strength and prosperity for John, Duane hugged him and said, "I love you, brother."

We walked to the car without a word. As Duane unlocked my door to let me in, he embraced me. "I just got out of prison!" he said.

After relinquishing that five thousand dollars, Duane's contracting business tripled. He had so many jobs he couldn't handle them all. I discovered a scripture years later that explained the spiritual principle that went into effect because Duane was willing to surrender his bitterness. "And the Lord turned the captivity of Job and restored his fortunes, when he prayed for his friends; also, the Lord gave Job twice as much as he had before" (Job 42:10 TAB).

Face and embrace your anger. Don't run from it or you'll crash. Keep on course. Trust that you'll get through the storm and find release. Think like this: *How can I express this rather than letting it fester inside? I need to let this out.*

Here are some ways we can deal with our anger constructively.

1. *Repeat in your mind that feelings are okay.* Feelings are not right or wrong, they just are. This includes anger. It's okay to feel angry.

2. *Talk, talk, talk.* Get your emotions out rather than keeping them inside. Sit down with some friends that you know you can depend on (more than one friend is advisable). Tell them how important it is for you to share your

feelings. Tell them what kind of response you need. If you need them to listen attentively and actively without giving advice, tell them you just need their ears to listen. Otherwise, some friends will turn you off because they don't know how to respond.

3. *If your friends are few, and you don't want to talk to them, talk into a tape recorder or write in your journal.* Find a warm fuzzy teddy bear and talk. Talk to *anything*, but talk!

4. *Find a support group.* A bond of similar experiences can be helpful.

5. *Repeat to yourself that it's okay to be angry.* You can be angry at whomever you want—the doctor, the minister, the one you lost, or God.

6. *Find physical activities to help you release your anger (or other emotions) outwardly.*

Try mowing the lawn, pulling weeds, working outside, or diving into some overdue painting projects. Sometimes it feels good to find an isolated place to scream. Praying often helps.

You will handle your anger in one (or two) of three ways: You will express it, repress it, or confess it.

To *express* it means to get your feelings out in the open or to rid yourself of them.

To *repress* it is to unconsciously push your feelings down deep into your subconscious because you can't or don't want to deal with them. Someday they will surface, probably in an unhealthy way.

To *confess* is to admit the way you feel. Confession helps you get rid of the anger and enables you to be forgiven.

Remember the man who borrowed the one thousand dollars right before Duane died? The story doesn't end with my anger. I learned a long time ago that when I was

81

having trouble loving someone, I needed to picture that person's face and circle it with love. Picturing this particular man's face was easy. But circling it with love was another matter. So I decided to be honest and circle it with anger. I literally fisted my hand, extended my pointing finger and drew large circles in the air around this guy's face. I circled fast and furiously complete with growling sound effects. I threw my whole body into this process because I was mad and needed to release my anger.

Months went by. I circled and circled and circled some more. Gradually, I sensed the anger disappear. Mysteriously, I began feeling pity and compassion for this man. I began circling his face with love. Real love. I wanted to love him and not become bitter, but it took time to get rid of the anger because my grief level was so high.

One day, nearly two years later, I decided to attend a church where I used to worship. It was Easter Sunday, and my friend and I were a little late. The church was packed out with only two seats back in the foyer in the middle of the row. We scooted in as quickly as possible. Just then, the pastor said, "Now, I'd like you to turn to the person on your right and the person on your left and tell them you love them and you're glad they're here."

I turned to my left. Lo and behold, the man I had circled for nearly two years turned to me in obvious shock. He began to stammer. Sweat poured down his reddening face. "Jjjjjoanne!" he managed to utter. "You look great."

I saw a pathetic, embarrassed man. Looking straight into his eyes, I said, "Charlie! I sure do love you, brother." He could hardly function. The next thing I knew the minister asked us to turn in our hymnals and sing.

Charlie got up and left. I've never seen him since. He's never returned the thousand dollars. But you know what? It doesn't matter. I didn't see a five hundred dollar bill in one eye and a five hundred dollar bill in his other eye. It didn't happen immediately, but I refused to let bitterness taint my life. God enabled me to completely dissipate my anger, forgive him, and circle him with love.

GUILT

Anger turned inward can become guilt. It hampers us, bogs us down, and makes us miserable. Like anger, guilt will not disappear just because we wish it away.

We must recognize guilt. Otherwise, it can cripple and prevent healing from taking place. Guilt can be one of the biggest challenges in getting through grief.

Two kinds of guilt are associated with grief. One has to do with unresolved relationships. Several years ago I met a young man who had an unresolved relationship with his father.

The first time we met was at his father's funeral. The service was rather unusual because the family sat behind partitions in the sanctuary. After the service, I returned to my office, which was situated so that you could use it for an alternate exit from the sanctuary. As I sat at my desk working, I heard this clanging noise descending the stairs. A man surrounded by two guards walked into my office, his hands and feet chained. He was sobbing uncontrollably. I stood to grab him and give him a hug.

"Don't touch him," snarled the guard.

I backed away, but I'll never forget the deep agony in his face as he passed through my office and disappeared into a police car. I can still hear those chains clanging.

Some months later as I co-hosted a late night radio program on the subject of grief, one of the callers asked to talk with me personally. His name was Brian, and he was calling from the state prison. He remembered me and asked if I would visit him and help him with his terrible guilt over the death of his father.

"Sure, I'll do the best I can to help you," I promised.

I cleared the necessary red tape and got word that I could go into prison. Visiting day arrived. I opened the iron gate to the visiting area and entered a holding room where I was frisked and given a pass. I began to wonder how I would recognize him among all these people.

The attendant called my name and Brian walked up to me. I recognized him immediately.

"You came, you came!" he said his eyes filling with hope.

"Of course. I said I would, didn't I?"

"Let's sit down over here," he suggested and then began to pour his heart out about feeling so guilty for his crimes and the pain that he had caused his family, particularly his late father. He talked about his grief for more than an hour. He was almost through his story when the guard bellowed, "Visiting hours are over. Time for you to leave, Ma'am."

"Oh, could we just have a few more minutes?" I pleaded.

"Well . . . okay," he conceded.

"Brian, I'd like to pray for you if it's all right with you," I offered.

"Oh, would you please?"

As I began to pray, big tears fell down his face, all the way to his shoes. As I said, "Amen," he looked up, radiant.

"I may be in prison, but I'm free from that horrible guilt. I can't thank you enough."

"Just seeing the peace on your face is thanks enough.

God bless you, Brian." I gave him a big hug and left.

When your guilt pertains to unresolved relationships, you need to forgive yourself. Are you willing to forgive yourself?

The second kind of guilt is connected with the circumstances surrounding a loved one's death.

Sam had a particularly tough time working through his guilt. Sam had grown up in an affluent but dysfunctional home. His mother had suffered from severe depression all Sam's life, but the family had done their best to conceal Mildred's problem from their friends. Whenever they had to commit her to a mental hospital, Sam and his father told friends she was away on a trip. Mildred was so depressed she often spoke of suicide.

Sam went away to college. His parents continued to have problems and dealt with them the American way—through recreation and alcohol. One day Sam's parents were having a party. All the guests drank heavily. Sam's father was so tipsy that he accidentally fell into the swimming pool while the other guests went in the house to eat. Nobody noticed Owen's absence until it was too late. Owen drowned.

Sam was devastated. His only link to parental stability died with the passing of his father. Mildred fell into a deep depression again, and she had to be committed to a psychiatric hospital.

Several months passed and Mildred improved. When she came home on a weekend pass from the hospital, she called Sam.

"Sam, I can't take it any longer. The hospital thinks I'm better but there's really no hope for me. I'm going to take my life."

"Oh, Mom, you don't really mean that. Now, c'mon,

85

cheer up. You've walked through this before, and you'll make it this time." Sam did his best to encourage his mom.

Two days later Sam got a call. "This is the Kansas City Police Department. Are you Sam Grant?"

"Yes. Why are you calling?"

"I'm sorry to inform you, Mr. Grant, but your mother, Mildred Grant, has committed suicide."

Sam's shock and horror were immediately compounded by tremendous guilt. "If only I'd taken her seriously. If only I'd checked on her or called a neighbor. She's threatened this for so many years, I never dreamed she would actually go through with it."

Remember, no relationship is ever perfect. Sometimes we say things in the heat of the moment that really hurt. We planned to resolve it after the anger subsided. But the disagreement did not get settled—our loved one died before we could forgive and receive forgiveness. Thoughts cross our minds: *If only Jim would have stopped and discussed this with me rationally before he left for work. If only I'd gone to the basketball game with him, instead of starting an argument, we could have worked through it before he died.* If only, if only, if only. The guilt floods in.

You had regular patterns for the way you handled disagreements in the relationship. If the loved one had not died, you would have moved the situation to a place of resolution. But the loved one has died. What now?

One way you know you have moved down the road to recovery is when you can see both the good and bad in the person you lost. Often we make perfect saints out of our lost loved ones and forget that they had any faults at all.

One suggestion is to write a letter to the loved one,

asking that person for forgiveness for the situation. Verbalizing and expressing your feelings will help you feel forgiven. Now you need to forgive yourself. Keep the letter or throw it away—the important thing is that you write it.

Sam wrote a letter to his mother and experienced release from his guilt. Many others have experienced similar successes with a "forgiveness letter."

When you get into the "I should have's" and "If only's," realize that grief is not logical—it's emotional! That's why answers from others don't always help. When you can believe you did all you could do—that it was something you had no control over, you are able to let go of the guilt.

But what if you were responsible? You may say, "I made the decision to end his life. I caused the accident—it was my fault." "I filed for the divorce." "I had the affair." This type of guilt is tougher to tackle. You will need help and a support system. If you continue to punish yourself, you will not only destroy yourself, but the wound will fester and you'll become bitter.

SAY GOODBYE TO YOUR GUILT TRIP

1. *Share your feelings of guilt.* Express them. Write them down in a journal.

2. *Deal with guilt feelings and bring them to resolution* so you can proceed with your healing. If you feel like you are rehearsing the same conversations in your mind, you may need to seek help to get out of the rut.

3. *Accept that what has happened has happened.* You cannot turn back the hands of time. If you were to blame, accept the blame. If it was an accident, accept it as an accident.

4. *Allow yourself to be forgiven.*

5. *Say goodbye* to the person and events surrounding the accident or divorce.

6. *Believe something good will come out of all this pain.*

7. *If you need further help, get a good grief counselor.*

8. *Remember, you can choose to become a bitter or better person.*

Forgiveness is giving up claim forever to the right of retaliation or compensation. Forgive yourself. Forgiveness is so important in moving toward healing. Don't nurse your grudge or rehearse it, but disperse it. Don't coddle the offense by feeding it or making it your bosom buddy. Don't rehearse it—don't play the offense over and over in your mind. Stop rationalizing your unforgiveness. Face it head on. Disperse it: detach yourself from the offense so that you're free to love the offender.

Ask yourself these questions to gauge whether or not you've truly forgiven.

1. *Am I comfortable around the person?*

2. *Can I have compassion for the person?*

3. *Can I think about the person without remembering the offense?*

If others won't forgive, that's their problem, not yours. If they won't forgive you, they must work that through to healing. At least you have done your part.

Expect a positive outcome. If you expect it, it will happen!

8

...

How to Say Goodbye: in Death

One goal in Grief Release is to withdraw the emotional energy we had invested in the relationship we lost by learning how to say goodbye to the relationship as it existed and can never exist again. Sometimes we see death coming and are able to say goodbye naturally.

I remember when my father died. He had succumbed to several strokes and was hospitalized. The doctors' prognosis gave us little hope. They said he had just a few hours to live and suggested that we remove the life support systems and let him quietly go.

I had to do some deep thinking about this and told the doctor I would let him know our decision.

We decided to remove all the paraphernalia except the IV's.

I wanted to stay with my father that night. One night

evolved into sixteen. I sat by his bed day after day, recalling the many sacrifices he made for me, the unselfish acts of love in a silent family.

I recited his favorite scripture—the Twenty-third Psalm. Then I signed it to him. Although he was deaf, I continued to talk to him and tell him how much I loved him. Unconsciously, I withdrew the emotional energy involved in a father/first-born daughter relationship. I remember making decisions from the age of ten; buying major appliances and counting out shoe money from the envelopes of our pigeonhole accounting system. We had a deep and unusual relationship because of his handicap.

During those sixteen days, I had an opportunity to say goodbye to my father. I let go.

Many times we don't get the opportunity to say goodbye. Then we need to create a goodbye. We never say goodbye to the good memories, we just acknowledge that the "relationship" is no longer there.

Many people have difficulty understanding this principle at a heart level. Think of it this way. When a child misbehaves, ideally we are "supposed" to separate the behavior from the person. Generally this ideal takes time to master. We've all heard "love the sinner and hate the sin." If the dysfunctional behavior runs rampant throughout the child's life, separating the person from hurtful deeds becomes increasingly difficult.

So it is with separating a relationship from a person. The only reason death hurts so badly is because of the relationship. The closer and more positive the relationship, the deeper the hole left by that person's absence.

Surprisingly, even in negative relationships, a hole still exists. This hole occurs mainly because of what "was not" or unfulfilled expectations. Expectations of "the perfect marriage," the "perfect mother," or "the perfect friend" wave an unrealistic banner of failure painted in large red letters. We see it every time we think of the person and recall the disappointments over and over until hopelessness settles in.

Either way, good or bad, we need to let go of the relationship and say goodbye before we can move on with our lives. Studies show that failure to release the relationship sows the seeds of pathology. Sick relationships abound in our culture because we have left unfinished business by failing to say goodbye. We want to move through life-changes quickly. But it is mandatory that we have an ending before any new beginnings can develop.

Say goodbye to unfulfilled expectations. You will make such headway when you hurdle this one. Psalm 48:13 tells us to "cease recalling disappointments" (TAB). The endless recalling of disappointments will forever hamper personal growth and sabotage your healing.

It's of utmost importance to take this procedure of saying goodbye bit by bit. Take one small part of the relationship at a time, and say goodbye to it.

Start your goodbye list with this question. "What do I miss doing the most with this person?"

With Duane, I missed going out to dinner as husband and wife, taking long walks together, having couples over for dessert, planning a "we" calendar, family vacations, and sexual intimacy.

After pondering all the activities you no longer enjoy with the person, separate the activities into categories. Title your list, "Saying goodbye to _____." As I reviewed what I missed sharing with Duane, my list included saying goodbye to:

- sports—golf, tennis, biking, and walking

- gardening
- social life
- vacations
- business
- church life and ministry
- mother-father relationship with our daughter
- marriage
- my best friend

As I made this list, I knew that I needed to start with something insignificant. I began with golf. Duane loved playing the game and sometimes wanted me to come along with him for company. I loved going with him, but every time he'd get ready to tee off, he'd turn to me and say, "Shhhh, Joanne. Be quiet. Shhhhh." I thought, *Well, it won't be too difficult for me to say goodbye to golf.*

I took one of the golf clubs out of the cart and put it right back in, and said goodbye to Duane and the relationship we had in golf. Then I sold the clubs. That wasn't too hard!

Under sports I wanted to say goodbye to our relationship in tennis. I got out his tennis racquet and recalled all the fun times we'd shared on the tennis court. We used to play before work, after work, and on weekends. Many times we took tennis vacations. My goal was always to beat him. But it didn't happen very often.

So I took his racquet and said, "Goodbye to the relationship we shared, Duane, in playing tennis."

Slowly, I put the tennis racquet away.

Choose a time to get rid of clothing and personal items. Keep at least one special item of that person's. At some time down the road, you will need that item of clothing or personal memento.

Amy kept one of Duane's work jackets. She wore it when she changed the oil on her car. She wore it for many months after Duane died. One day I saw it in the closet, brought it out, and said to Amy, "My goodness, this jacket has gotten really dirty. I think I'd better wash it."

"Oh, Mom, don't do that," she pleaded. "It still smells like Dad."

And so, as you're saying goodbye to the relationship as it existed and can no longer exist, keep some piece of clothing just as a reminder of the person you love and are letting go of.

Take as much time as you need to work through these different areas in your grief. I remember when I was ready to say goodbye to our relationship in gardening. Duane loved to start plants from seeds and grow them in our back bedroom and in the garage.

Our garden was on our deck. Duane placed tubs in the corners of the deck and planted tulip bulbs in them. I remembered picking out colors for each of the tubs. The spring after Duane's death when the tulips began to bloom, I knelt down and recalled all the fun times we had working in our tub garden. I sat next to each one of those tubs and let the tears flow down my face. I said goodbye to my wonderful gardening friend. I released that part of our relationship.

After saying goodbye to planting tulips, I waited a while. The key to saying goodbye is doing it slowly, thoroughly, and one step at a time.

Next I worked through saying goodbye to our social life, vacations, business life, and church life.

When I reached the point of saying goodbye to our relationship as parents, I remembered how devastated we were when we discovered we couldn't bear children. I remembered the grief. And finally, the decision to adopt a child.

One night when I returned from a shopping trip, Duane raced out to meet me in the driveway.

"Joanne, guess what? We have a baby girl. Our daughter was born while you were shopping."

When three-day-old Amy was placed into Duane's arms, she looked up at Duane and smiled.

"She already knows me," he said proudly.

I recalled our parenting years and some of the tough times during Amy's teens. As I said goodbye to the relationship we shared as parents and let go of it, I realized that relationship could no longer exist.

Several weeks passed before I was ready to start saying goodbye to our marriage. I realized I needed to say goodbye to the sexual part of our relationship. I went back to our bedroom, the place I was now sleeping all alone. I knelt down next to the bed and cried out to God. "God, I need your help. I'm asking you to cap off all my sexual feelings. Would you come in and touch them?"

You know what, he did. The gift of celibacy covered all those feelings as I let go of them. I believe that someday if I re-marry those feelings will be released so I can love fully and purely.

Next, as a part of saying goodbye to the marriage I needed to remove my wedding rings. I went back in my memory bank to the time when Duane asked me to become his wife.

We were both home from college that weekend. I remember saying to him, "Yes, I want to live the rest of my life with you."

Duane made arrangements for us to visit our favorite jeweler. He told him how much money he had and that he wanted to buy his future wife her engagement and wedding rings.

We arrived at the jewelry store full of anticipation.

As we sat down, the jeweler opened a beautiful velvet case displaying a dazzling collection of rings within Duane's price range. I remember how excited we were as we looked at all these rings.

What fun we had as we admired the different rings on my hand. Finally, I made my choice.

As soon as we exited the shop, we fell into each other's arms and hugged and kissed because we were so excited. On the night of our engagement party, Duane gave me the engagement ring in the center of an orchid.

He said, "I love you. I can hardly wait to become your husband."

The days flew by, and it was time for the wedding. I remember the moment in the ceremony when Duane put the rings on my hand and said, "I love you for better or for worse, for richer or for poorer, in sickness and in health, 'til death do us part."

'Til death do us part, I thought. *We've parted. I'm no longer married. The relationship that I had is over. Death has parted us.* I looked down at my hand and, with tears filling my eyes, I slowly took the rings off of my finger. For the first time in twenty-five years I was not married. I was not wearing rings. I felt so vulnerable and afraid. A feeling of nakedness overcame me. As I put the rings in the dresser I thought, *There has to be a way to walk through this, let go of those rings, and still hold onto the memory.*

After a few weeks, I consulted a jeweler about the diamonds in my wedding and engagement ring. I asked him to help me create a ring using those same diamonds.

I now wear the "memory" ring to acknowledge twenty-five years of marriage, a precious reminder of what Duane and I shared.

You see, working through the concept of saying

goodbye to the relationship as it existed and can no longer exist gives you an opportunity to let go of what has been, but also gives you the freedom to never forget the good memories and what you shared together.

When I finished working through the various sub-headings under marriage, I knew I was ready for the final goodbye. I chose to do it in the cemetery. You could choose to do it anywhere.

I arrived at the cemetery wearing a new dress in one of Duane's favorite colors. I went to the florist and bought a bouquet of his favorite flowers.

As I stepped up to the marker, the stark reality of seeing his name in granite overwhelmed me. I thought, *Duane R. Smith—that name has meant so much to me over the last years.*

"I came today, Duane, to say a final goodbye to our relationship as best friends. Oh, you were such a good friend to me. You understood my heartbeat. You listened to my heartbeat. You did everything you could to release me. Thank you for being such a good listener. Oh, how I miss that. Thank you for the intimate talks when you shared your dreams with me—dreams you never shared with anyone else. I kept those dreams close to my heart. I remember the long quiet walks . . . the times when we didn't know if you were going to live . . . the pain when you were recovering from open-heart surgery. Oh, I have so many memories. I thank you that I don't have to say goodbye to the memories, but I need to let go.

"Today my precious friend, I come to say goodbye. Goodbye, goodbye. I will always love you. But I come to release the relationship and say goodbye. Goodbye, best friend. Goodbye."

Grief is the price you pay for the ability to love.

HOW TO WALK THROUGH SEXUAL
WITHDRAWAL

Here are some tips for saying goodbye to the sexual part of your marriage. I found that my sexual feelings didn't die just because Duane did. One day he was a vital part of my life and the next day he was gone. I searched for someone to tell me how to resolve the inner urges. The world's answer was unacceptable to me as a woman of integrity so I asked God to help me.

1. *Go before God and ask him to cap sexual feelings.* Ask God to give you a gift of celibacy. I merely sat down next to my bed and cried out to God, "Father, I don't know what to do with all the feelings of love I used to express to Duane. Could you just come down and touch those feelings and take away my sexual desires or show me how to cope with them?" He will. He did it for me. It's a delicate issue and difficult to describe, but he touches those vulnerable places.

2. *Be careful about TV and movie consumption.* Even after your sexual feelings are capped off, you can willfully undo the cap. Watching TV and movies with sexual scenes or innuendos will immediately open you up to attack. Stick to family entertainment.

3. *When around "lovey-dovey" people, excuse yourself and leave.* Just as watching lovemaking on the screen triggers a reaction in you, kissing friends can trigger the same reaction. Don't be pious or uppity about it, just quietly move to another location until the smoochers are finished.

4. *Use a heating pad at night for warmth.* After sleeping for nearly twenty-five years with a human hot water bottle, I nearly froze at night. I discovered that going to bed with a heating pad helped immensely. I followed the

precautions on the instruction sheet, and Mr. Heating Pad and I became fast nocturnal friends.

5. *Refuse to listen to details about others' sexual activities.* If counseling a friend, set ground rules. Ask the person to avoid the juicy tidbits. Hearing as well as seeing can lead to fantasizing and blow away the caps.

6. *Be cautious about body language when around the opposite sex by giving and receiving "heart-centered" hugs only.* Most people can sense the difference between heart-centered and sexually-enticing hugs. Make sure you communicate the heart-centered kind.

7. *Get a massage.* The professional touch of a licensed massage therapist can somewhat relieve the skin hunger experienced by most people whose spouses die. Some chiropractors also give great massages.

SAYING GOODBYE TO A CHILD

Perhaps you have lost a child. I've worked with grieving parents of every imaginable mode of death from murder, car accidents, victims of drunk drivers, freak farm and recreational accidents, Sudden Infant Death Syndrome, miscarriage, and stillborn births. The goodbye lists are as varied as the children were unique.

When saying goodbye to a child, place your hands together, palms up. Envision holding your child in your hands. Slowly raise your child up to heaven, separate your hands like you're releasing a fledgling bird to fly. Now say, "Goodbye, Stacy, goodbye." This simple physical exercise aids the heart act of saying goodbye. Your list may include saying goodbye to:
- your nurturing role
- school and athletic activities
- Mother's Day and Father's Day cards
- shared dreams, future plans

98

- family vacations minus one
- buying school clothes
- messy rooms
- tons of dirty clothes
- shopping without buying certain favorite foods
- dinner table minus one
- tied-up telephones
- spontaneous laughter of a houseful of kids

Some women become stalemated in the goodbye process because of a prior unresolved loss. Unsettled issues of abortion usually arise at this time. After learning about the many types of loss, an unidentifiable unsettledness gnaws at them. They can't quite understand why an apparently insignificant loss is causing them so much difficulty.

When I discuss the issue of abortion in grief classes, I do not approach it from a moral viewpoint, but only from its association to grief. Women can immediately see that the loss they thought they were addressing was really a secondary loss. Their primary loss was rooted in a prior abortion.

Whether or not the women consented to the abortion by coercion, ignorance, or choice, none of them were prepared for the emotional aftermath. After facing this loss, these women suffer serious regrets.

In the counseling room, I've met women who have later deeply wanted a baby and either miscarried or were unable to conceive because of prior abortions. Abortion compounds grief and forms layers of complicated issues to unravel.

In saying goodbye to an unborn child, include all the relevant issues and expectations you would have for planned children. Some women name their aborted children and write letters to them asking for forgiveness.

A sample goodbye list for a parent or close friend may include:

- shared secrets
- meals out
- shopping
- exchanging gifts
- trips
- long talks
- hugs

When saying goodbye to a relationship terminated by suicide, try expressing your love in a letter on thin paper to the person. List all the reasons why you'll miss the person. Attach the letter to the tail of a mylar helium balloon. You may want to select that person's favorite color. Go to a meaningful place, say your goodbyes, and release the balloon, watching it disappear into the sky.

Whatever the cause of death, your goodbye list should include all those activities you can no longer share with that special person.

Even after you think you've completely worked through your goodbyes, you will inevitably happen upon a "trigger" place you omitted from your list. But eventually, you will exhaust all the "memory spots"—places you visited with your loved one and haven't frequented since the death.

Time does not heal all wounds. Saying goodbye and letting go will patch that horrible hole in your heart— slowly, steadily, surely, it will happen.

9
...

How to Say Goodbye to the Living: Divorce, Broken Relationships, Relocation, Empty Nests

As I said in Chapter 8, one goal in Grief Release is to withdraw the emotional energy we had invested in the relationship we lost. We must say goodbye to the relationship as it existed and can never exist again. Often this involves saying goodbye to someone who is still alive but is no longer a part of our daily lives.

Losses that mean saying goodbye to the living include divorce, broken relationships, relocation, empty-nest syndrome, and serious changes in our health or that of someone we love.

In dealing with divorce, many suffer from anger and hurt. Because divorce surfaces feelings rooted in rejection and jealousy, when saying goodbye to a marriage, it is easier to write out the goodbye and read it aloud. The outward verbal expression helps a person work through the hurt and anger more effectively.

Here's what one woman wrote in her goodbye to her husband:

- Goodbye to my fear of abandonment. Being alone is better than being with someone who magnifies your aloneness.
- Goodbye to walking on eggs—being afraid of doing something wrong.
- Goodbye to the pain of rejection in my bed.
- Goodbye to his anger toward women.
- Goodbye to his temper and bad language.
- Goodbye to his coldness to me.
- Goodbye to his unfulfilled promises and empty words.
- Goodbye to his bills I helped him pay.
- Goodbye to his unwillingness to walk with me and enjoy me.
- Goodbye to the power I let him have in my life.
- Goodbye to the energy I expended trying to please him.
- Goodbye to being seated next to him in church.
- Goodbye to his smile and hugs.
- Goodbye to the gentle man, the little boy that I once knew who left me when we got married.
- Goodbye to the dreams.
- Goodbye to being his wife until I die.

- Hello to having more time to spend with God.
- Hello to peace within me.
- Hello to the time I am gaining to spend with my daughter.
- Hello to healing.
- Hello to my many new friends.

- Hello to a reprieve rather than mental bondage for the rest of my life.
- Hello to being able to understand what it is I need to beware of in men and myself.

She actually moved her goodbyes to hellos.

To discover some tips for saying goodbye to the sexual part of your marriage, re-read the section entitled "How to Walk Through Sexual Withdrawal" on page 97.

Goodbyes are as different as the people saying them. Here's one involving a broken male-female relationship:

Dear Jason,

I dread this moment but have to face it squarely. I feel as if I'm sitting next to you in the train at the airport again. This time, however, the heaviness in my heart is so much greater because I feel as if I've known you for such a long, long time.

I don't know what to say except that I have enjoyed knowing you as a friend. You're a fun person to be with. Oh . . . you made me laugh and you made me talk.

You seemed to know so much of me within a short time. Your perceptiveness made me curious. You seemed too deep to comprehend.

When we talked about our future and when you said you'd like to support me in my future and even wished to be a part of it, I felt as if we could ride this train together forever. Nonetheless, the reality is that our journey together has to end sooner than we'd expected.

Obviously you have your responsibilities to carry on, and I have my work to do, too. It's sad that we have to part so soon—separated by time and space. However, I thank you for all the good memories you've left with me. It is certainly encouraging to know that people like you exist.

I hope your fiance and you will be able to overcome the difficulties you have in communication. I wish for God's best for both of you. Although I haven't met her personally, I believe she must be a beautiful woman. I'm happy for you. She is very fortunate. You obviously have paid quite a high cost for your relationship with her. Perhaps some day I'll get to meet her. Then, perhaps we could all be friends.

Goodbye, my friend. Goodbye. May our Lord bless you with his very best.

From your friend,
Andrea

The freedom of our mobile society brings with it great sorrow when friends move away. Part of the grief involves the lack of instant accessibility to treasured friends. Although we can pick up the telephone, new and unfamiliar environments take their toll in accentuating our loneliness.

Judy remembers moving from southern California to northern Oregon. Since she lived in the same small town from birth to marriage, she enjoyed plenty of life-long friends. All her family and roots were deeply embedded in "home." After college and marriage, she moved seventeen times in a few years including to Germany, Texas, and Georgia. She ultimately ended up in a rural community in Oregon. She didn't know one person outside of her immediate family, three of whom were under the age of eight. Her husband went off happily every day to his new job in "God's country," while she acquainted children with new schools and tried to re-establish her life. She suffered deep depression even though she was grateful for the clean air, new friends, and fresh opportunities. Relocation, whether welcomed or not, involves grief.

Her goodbye went something like this:

- Goodbye to mother and father, sister and family.
- Goodbye to familiar places and faces.
- Goodbye to church and ministry positions.
- Goodbye to piano students.
- Goodbye to the safety of knowing who to call for help.
- Goodbye to sunshine.
- Goodbye to smog.
- Goodbye to long phone conversations.
- Goodbye to Disneyland.
- Goodbye to Pic 'n Save and Marie Callender's Restaurant.

The transition that takes place when children become adults tears at the heartstrings of moms everywhere. A painful goodbye occurs when children leave home. Whether the time is right or not, the sudden absence of a child causes maternal grief.

One woman shared that every time she walked past her son's room she cried. Whenever she saw his friends on the road or at a school function, her heart sank and a surge of loneliness crashed over her. She bought his brand of cereal, set his place for dinner, called one of her other children by his name. Change is never easy.

Her goodbye went like this:

- Goodbye to his big brown eyes.
- Goodbye to his friendly outgoing manner.
- Goodbye to his hugs.
- Goodbye to meetings at the school.

- Goodbye to sibling feuds.
- Goodbye to late night "watching and waiting."

International families walk through a painful goodbye when working in one country and leaving children in another. Such factors as political unrest and expensive plane fares add to the anxiety level of families split by continents and oceans.

One mother going on a ten-year overseas commitment had to leave a college-age son, Eric, as well as her newly married son, Nathan. Although she had sent both sons to boarding schools every year, this goodbye was of a more permanent nature.

I suggested she bring some stones, a picture of each of her sons, and two letters describing all the aspects of the relationship they would no longer share. We chose a lovely park with a lake. We walked and she talked about how much she loved her sons. She was close to both of them as they grew up as a tight-knit family in Eastern Africa.

After we located an especially lovely and private spot, she began to build two small altars with the stones. As she placed stone upon stone, she spoke about the character qualities she appreciated in first Eric, then Nathan. After the altar was completed, she placed the picture of each boy on the altar. One after the other, we prayed prayers of relinquishment as she held up their pictures to the Lord. We then walked over to the lake where she threw each rock into the water, completing her commitment of goodbye.

Whether your parting is caused by happy or painful circumstances, be sure to say goodbye. I give the gift of closure whenever I learn that a friend or someone in our support group is leaving. I acknowledge the friendship, tell how much the person has meant to me, and how much I'll miss her. In a group setting, I ask the person to share about the future and the benefits as well as the hard places involved in the move. I then give opportunity for the class to share in the goodbye. The gift of closure seals the gift of friendship and leaves an open door for easy return.

10

...

Developing a Support System: "If There's Anything I Can Do . . ."

"Hello, Barbara?" the voice carefully inquired. "This is Marcia. I'm so sorry to hear about your loss. If there's anything I can do for you, anything at all, *pulleeze*, don't hesitate to call me."

"Thank you, Marcia, but I can't think of a thing," Barbara answered in a monotone. "Goodbye." She sounded as if she were in a daze.

WHY A SUPPORT SYSTEM?

Support means to hold up or in position; to bear the weight or stress of; to keep from sinking or falling; also, to sustain a load. *System* is defined as an organized whole. A support system is a group of somebodies who love us and will come alongside us to help sustain the stressful load caused by grief.

A support system consists of a network of people, usually two to ten, who have committed themselves to lend a hand in practical ways.

A support system provides a reason to stay stable. A support system will help stabilize you by functioning as a sounding board. You need familiar surroundings during the transition of loss.

Grief is the hardest work you'll ever do. You can't move through it alone. You need help. Even the most "together," organized, stable, normal person needs help when it comes to releasing grief. The grief process is not meant to be a solitary journey. Many people never fully release grief because they refuse the help of their friends and family.

A support system is not a cleaning service, a therapist, a slave market, an easy-out, or a cure-all. It is caring, loving people who are available to help you—physically, emotionally, and spiritually. Some people sabotage their own potential support systems by whining, self-pity, and manipulation. If you're honest, vulnerable, and willing to take responsibility for yourself, people will want to help you.

One way to develop a support system is to locate a community support group relating to your specific type of loss. Call your church, United Way, or local college.

HOW TO BUILD A SUPPORT SYSTEM

So, how do you begin to build this support system?

Recruit people who are patient, discreet, and available. Don't depend on only one person to help you through this time. You'll wear out one person. Find several who are available around the clock.

Engage a friend to be your support coordinator. Let's say her name is Susie. Sit down with Susie and let her ask

110

you questions about your needs. Be specific. Make sure Susie knows you well enough so that she can discern the heartfelt helpers from the nosy meddlers. If you are presently unable to interact with certain people, tell Susie. You won't want to spend all day at home with Gertrude if she makes you nervous.

When people call and offer to help, ask them to call Susie.

If people want to bring food, be honest enough when accepting help to say, "We've already had tuna six times this week, but we'd be glad to eat just about anything else."

You may need assistance in manual labor, financial advice, emotional encouragement, or counseling. Write down your needs and tell your support system. If you're a perfectionist, leave household repairs or heavy cleaning to the professionals. By doing this, you won't become angry when your support system fails to meet your expectations. Don't get defensive by complaining, "My friends are letting me down."

When your friends ask if you need help, say yes. Don't withdraw from caring people. Select people from different age brackets. Find people from work, church, your neighborhood, and/or family.

Sit down and tell your support team some specifics. I needed to receive encouraging mail every day. Just after Duane died, the following letter arrived:

Joanne:
Hello! We've never met, but I'm sure it would be a pleasure for me if you are a reflection of Duane and his values and standards.

I sold appliances and knew Duane in that capacity. He *always* brought joy into my day, and I looked forward to his visits. Often, we would discuss everything under the sun. I especially enjoyed our conversations about the Lord. I don't know the circumstances of Duane's passing, but I'm sure he's at home with the Lord. His life, as I saw it, demonstrated a joyful working out (yes, real application) of Christianity.

I will miss him, too. Our family will support you and Amy in prayer, Joanne. I hope you will be able to feel it.

In his love,
Don

EMOTIONAL SUPPORT

For the first several weeks after Duane died, I went to my mailbox every day only to find bills and junk mail. Finally, I asked five women to write a card to me each week for eight weeks. I even told them what to say and the specific day I wanted the card to arrive. The script went like this: Dear Joanne, you are going to make it! I love you.

Hugs are important! I so missed Duane's big old bear hugs. To help ease the pain, I hand-picked some trustworthy men from our church. After getting permission from their wives, I asked each man to commit to giving me a heart-centered hug whenever we met. They were glad to oblige.

On the lighter side, following are some therapeutic facts about hugging. Heart-centered hugs banish loneliness and demand no special setting (anyplace from an executive conference room to a church). Hugs help overcome fears—we feel secure when our arms are wrapped around somebody. Hugs make a happy day happier and make impossible days possible. Hugs get us in touch with our feelings and build self-esteem ("You really want to hug me?"). Hugging imparts a sense of belonging, eases tensions, fills up emptiness in our lives, is democratic (everyone qualifies for a hug), and keeps benefiting us even after the hug is released. Hugging attacks insomnia and feels so good.

In *A Book of Hugs* by Dave Ross we read, "Never hug tomorrow someone you could hug today."[1] In *More Hugs*, Dr. Virginia Satir states, "Four hugs a day are necessary for survival, eight are good for maintenance, and twelve for growth."[2]

Indoctrinate your support system on the subject of mood swings and grief. You will certainly experience them. You'll be emotinally up and down. You will have good days, bad days, and trigger times—a sudden depression caused by some stimulus reminding you of the loved one.

On some days you will wish you could hoist a flag or send up smoke signals announcing, "Today I need to be alone" or "Today I need company." Learn to understand yourself well enough to communicate specific needs to your support system. Watch for patterns in your grief— specific times of day or certain routines triggering waves of grief. Prepare ahead of time for these by forewarning your support system.

One day in my early grief, I sat in a restaurant eating lunch with an old friend. Unexpectedly, a dark cloud of depression descended over me. I began to cry. My friend became uncomfortable. She expected me to be "up," but I couldn't muster even a smile. Thereafter I tried to match my moods to my social calendar. I needed to be able to say both "yes" and "no" and not be overwhelmed by invitations. I had to decide when I was emotionally strong enough for social luncheons and when I was not.

Special Occasions or Events

During the first year of grief, don't go alone to such

celebrations as weddings, twenty-fifth wedding anniversaries, etc. Even if you think you're strong and emotionally stable, ask someone to go with you.

SPIRITUAL SUPPORT

Share your spiritual needs with someone you respect and trust. When you disclose personal prayer requests, make them short-term and specific. Be sure to go back and express your appreciation for the prayers, especially when the results are evident.

When people are praying for you, you will feel the difference. Your own spiritual resources may feel totally depleted because of grief-induced numbness. Extra prayer support will help carry you through this difficult time.

In Grief Release classes we have a hidden support system—a group of intercessors who each take a name from the class list and pray for one person for five weeks. We see amazing results at the end of the five weeks.

Join a Bible study. Whether or not you're able to function at full capacity, just be there and soak it up. Make sure the group is committed to loving and accepting you without expectations of performance.

FINANCIAL SUPPORT

For financial advice, seek out a professional financial consultant who has been personally recommended *and* thoroughly checked out by someone you trust. Grieving people need sound financial direction.

PHYSICAL NEEDS SUPPORT

One of my neighbors asked what my needs were just after Duane died.

"I really need a walking partner," I admitted.

"I'd be willing to walk every morning—Monday

through Friday. I'll be there, walk with you, and listen to you without prying. If you just need me to let you cry or talk or whatever, I'm committed to you," she offered.

So rain or shine, summer or winter, we walked. For the first year, I cried. She passed me the Kleenex, sometimes wrapped her arm around me, and gently supported me. What a practical and loving gift of support she was and still is.

INANIMATE SUPPORT

Buy a new book. See it as a new friend. Invest extra time in this "inanimate" support system. I enjoyed the wonderful gift of reading.

Talk to a picture of your lost loved one. Sometimes it helps to look at the person while you're working through your grief. Talk about your feelings just as if you were carrying on a conversation.

Music has long been used in mood therapy. Saul used to ask David to soothe his anxious heart by playing the harp. Try the following to help lift you out of depression: Beethoven's Piano Concerto No. 5 (Emperor), Dvorak's Symphony No. 8, Handel's choruses from the Messiah, Rachmaninoff's Piano Concerto No. 2 (last movement), and Mendelssohn's Symphony No. 4 (Italian).

Classical music soothes and motivates rather than triggers emotions as pop songs may tend to do. You might have a friend with similar musical tastes who would be willing to record or compile some "mood music" to help comfort your wounded spirit. We call it music therapy.

Because of the full range of emotions in David's writings, listening to tapes of the Psalms provides a balm for hurting hearts. Tapes are available in all versions—choose your favorite.

115

Since self-esteem is eroded in the grief process, let your support system affirm you. Give them the character qualities on pages 117-118 and ask them to list your positive traits. If this requires too much courage, hand them the book and let them read this section.

The essence of who you are has *not* been obliterated by your loss. As you cooperate with embracing the grief process, your positive character qualities will deepen. You will have grown as an individual and contributing member of society. This is merely a "time-out" in your life. At this point, you are primarily concerned with emotional survival rather than long-range meaning in your life. But take this small step. It will bridge the gap between who you actually are and who you thought you were prior to the loss.

Make a list of your positive qualities. Don't listen to your feelings on this one. Remember the "normal" person you were before the loss.

After you have completed your list, tape it to your bathroom mirror and read it to yourself every morning. Add any additional qualities your support system saw in you to your list.

"Without a vision the people perish" (Prov. 29:18 KJV). Focusing on the real person God created in you will facilitate your healing. Repetition aids in the learning process. As you see the "vision" of your God-given attributes and those you've developed with his supervision, the scales of grief will slowly sluff off from your eyes.

In Psalm 139 we read, "O Lord, you have searched me and you know me. . . For you created my inmost being; you knit me together in my mother's womb. I praise you because I am fearfully and wonderfully made; your works are wonderful, I know that full well" (Ps. 139:1, 13, 14).

As your needs change, tell your support system. As

A PICTURE OF ME—I AM . . .

Able	Compassionate	Free
Above-board	Competent	Friendly
Accepting	Concise	Fun
Active	Concerned	Generous
Adaptable	Confident	Genial
Adventurous	Conscientious	Gentle
Affectionate	Consistent	Giving
Agreeable	Considerate	Godly
Alert	Content	Graceful
Ambitious	Co-operative	Grateful
Appreciative	Courageous	Growing
Artistic	Courteous	Happy
Assertive	Creative	Healthy
Attentive	Devoted	Honest
Attractive	Dignified	Honorable
Authentic	Diligent	Hospitable
Available	Direct	Humble
Aware	Discerning	Imaginative
Bold	Disciplined	Independent
Brave	Discreet	Industrious
Bright	Effervescent	Informed
Broad-minded	Efficient	Ingenious
Calm	Encouraging	Innocent
Caring	Enduring	Innovative
Certain	Energetic	Insightful
Cheerful	Enthusiastic	Keen-eyed
Classy	Extroverted	Learned
Clean	Fair	Lighthearted
Clever	Faithful	Likable
Colorful	Flexible	Lively
Comfortable	Forgiving	Logical
Committed	Frank	Loving

117

A PICTURE OF ME—I AM . . . (continued)

Loyal
Mature
Meek
Mellow
Merciful
Merry
Modest
Moral
Musical
Natural
Neat
Nice
Non-judgmental
Objective
Observant
Open
Optimistic
Organized
Original
Patient
Peaceful
Peacemaker
Persistent
Persuasive
Playful
Pleasant
Poetic
Polite

Positive
Precise
Predictable
Principled
Punctual
Radiant
Rational
Reasonable
Reassuring
Realistic
Relaxed
Reverent
Romantic
Satisfied
Scientific
Secure
Self-accepting
Self-assured
Self-aware
Self-controlled
Self-reliant
Self-respecting
Sensible
Sensitive
Serious
Sincere
Skillful
Sociable

Spontaneous
Stable
Steadfast
Straightforward
Strong
Stylish
Successful
Supportive
Sympathetic
Tactful
Talented
Teachable
Tender
Thorough
Thoughtful
Thrifty
Tolerant
Trustworthy
Truthful
Understanding
Unselfish
Useful
Verbal
Virtuous
Visionary
Warm
Well-mannered

you progress in the healing process, the confusion and lethargy will lift. You will need less support in some areas. Take your time. Often grieving people fear losing the warmth and love of doting friends and perpetuate their grief. If you're really working through this grief process and are committed to getting well, this will not happen to you. Realize that your friendships will only deepen as you grow.

11

...

Learning to Listen: Hearing Aids for the Heart

I was sitting, torn by grief. Someone came and talked to me of God's dealings, of why it happened, of hope beyond the grave. He talked constantly. He said things I knew were true.

I was unmoved, except to wish he'd go away. He finally did.

Another came and sat beside me. He didn't talk. He didn't ask me leading questions. He just sat beside me for an hour and more, listened when I said something, answered briefly, prayed simply, and left. I was moved. I was comforted. I hated to see him go.[1]

One of the greatest cries I hear from people of all ages and types of trauma is "Help! I feel like I'm drowning." Or

"I need someone to talk to who really understands. People are all around me, but nobody's listening."

The number one challenge in our world today is loneliness. Remember that being real is the S.O.S. of healing in releasing grief. The first "S" is for Sharing (feelings, confusion, failure, frustrations, fears—those emotions trapped inside of you). The "O" is for Openness (honesty, vulnerability), and the other "S" represents Sensitivity to your own needs.

Now take what you've learned and offer your ears to a hurting someone. Even though you're not totally well yourself, you know how crucial good listeners are to emotional healing. Toss out the S.O.S. lifeline to someone else. Listening is the most important skill in helping the hurting. "Be quick to listen, slow to speak and slow to get angry" (James 1:19). We have two ears, two eyes, and one mouth. Perhaps we should listen more than we talk. A good listener is caring, compassionate, tolerant, and highly esteems the other person.

Listening involves looking at the speaker. If you can sit close to the person and look into his or her face, do. Reach out, touch your friend's hand, or, better yet, give a hug. Focusing on your friend shows that you care and are ready to listen.

Listen intently and lean toward the speaker. Your primary reason for listening is not to gather information about the problem but to listen to the person. As the feelings spill out, you'll also pick up information about the problem. But solving the problem is not your primary goal.

Think of yourself as an empty bucket. As your friend pours all of his or her feelings into you, don't interrupt. Keep your mouth closed. Let the person talk. A bucket doesn't respond with Bible verses or great insights. The gift you're offering is your ears. The best counselors are the ones who say the least.

The process of listening means that you keep focusing on your friend. While looking into your friend's eyes, nod to indicate that you understand what is being said. You might say, "Uh, huh." "Yes, yes, I hear you." These phrases encourage sharing without offering evaluations.

You may need to assist your friend to continue emptying feelings into your bucket. When your friend stops talking, just sit quietly, reach out, and gently touch an arm. Sometimes people need silence to think through what they're saying and what's happening to them. Listening ears allow room for silence while the other person is thinking and trying to form the words. Don't be afraid of silence.

It might also be helpful to rephrase the last idea that your friend spoke in the form of a question. For example, your friend may say, "Bruce says that we should have never gotten married."

You wait a few moments and then quietly ask, "Bruce feels your marriage was a mistake from the beginning?" A question allows your friend the privilege to continue talking.

The purpose of your listening is to drain off your friend's emotions—to help get feelings and ideas out front. It gives you an opportunity to join in the hurt and to bear the problem with your friend. Galatians 6:2, 3 verifies this: "Carry each other's burdens, and in this way you will fulfill the law of Christ. If anyone thinks he is something when he is nothing, he deceives himself." Remember that helpful listening is hard work.

When the person seems finished talking, say, "Have you said all you need to say? Would you like to add anything?" These enabling questions allow the person to share more.

123

These four steps will help you become the kind of listener people will want to confide in.

1. *Don't probe.* A thin line exists between listening and probing—but an important one. To listen is to enable others to say all they want to say. To probe is to make others share what they do not want to say and should not reveal at this time. A probing question takes away the initiative from the person who's sharing.

I remembered the young woman who came to me one day, agonizing over something she'd held onto for many years. She needed me to listen to her. She hadn't told anyone else.

"Okay," I encouraged her.

She opened up her heart and then shared something that had happened to her long ago. I sat on the edge of my seat, captivated by what she was telling me. As she got into the most intense part of the story, she began to cry. Then, suddenly, she stopped speaking and sobbed.

"Do you have anything else you want to add?" I asked.

She just looked up at me. "No."

Inside, I thought to myself, *No! You mean to tell me that you've brought me to this part of the story, and you don't need to tell me the rest? You've said all you need to say?*

I put my arm around her and said, "Just let me pray for you."

After we finished praying, she smiled and said, "Thanks! I'm a lot better. I feel great." She got up, gave me a hug, and left.

I never did hear the rest of the story, but it didn't matter. She shared just what she wanted to share and no more.

2. *Don't give advice.* It is important that we own our own problems and the solutions. Therefore, we must be

careful not to give any direct advice. The cheapest thing in the world is advice. Often the person with the least information is the most free with advice. The results can be disastrous. Instead, ask, "What do you think?" "What are your options?" "What are your feelings about this problem?"

Remember, if you ask these questions too early, your friend will think you are only problem-oriented and that you don't care about him or her as a person.

3. *Help her own the problem.* As your friend talks about the problem, listen for a sense of ownership. Suppose you're trying to help a woman whose husband left her. In the early stages, she may deny that it has happened. She may say he'll come back to his senses. She may project blame on several different people because of what she feels they did. As long as she blames or denies that it has happened, she has not owned the problem.

If she strongly denies the problem, continue to listen. Help her verbalize her bitter, angry feelings. Eventually, she will admit, "Well, I guess he's really not coming back. What am I going to do about it?" Now that she's owned the problem, she's ready to move forward in her healing.

4. *Don't judge.* Helpful listening does not judge nor criticize. It does not teach nor exhort. Most of all, helpful listening is not conversation.

Put your love to the test. When you violently disagree with others, can you give them the right to their own viewpoint? Do you not only affirm others, but release them to be themselves and to think as they must? This does not mean giving in or making concessions. It simply means telling them, "I cannot see it your way, but I love you and accept you just as you are with what you believe."

When this kind of listening and caring, loving acceptance happens, you will participate in the healing of someone's life. You will be tossing the lifeline of sharing ears to a sinking someone. You become a lifesaver.

WHEN IT'S TIME TO HELP WITH SOLUTIONS . . .

Work together on solutions. Say to your friend, "Let's talk about some of your options. Let's brainstorm. If you could do anything you wanted to, what would you do? Let's list every possible option." Your role now is to help your friend get a broad perspective on every possibility.

After all the possible solutions are out in front, ask for more about each solution. "What do you think about each option? More importantly, how do you feel about it?" Now you are encouraging your friend not only to own the problem, but also to own any solution that will come.

Use every opportunity to affirm. Put these practical phrases into your vocabulary: "You are valuable to me." Or "I believe in you; you're going to make it." If you've had a similar experience, share it. Give compliments every day. Smile and be enthusiastic whether you feel like it or not.

As you reach out, admit your honest feelings. If your friend's sharing stuns you, say so. If you are overwhelmed with compassion, admit it. If you suddenly feel tears coming, cry. Even if you are a Christian with a firm hope in the hereafter, you are also human. Don't hide that. It may be through this gate as you are real that a stronger friendship will develop.

Put yourself in the other person's shoes. When you become a lifesaver you are able to reach out into your world and give something of yourself away.

To do this, we must first learn the difference between sympathy and empathy. If I don't learn this distinction, I will be ineffective in the helping role.

Sympathy is over-involvement in the emotion of another person. Sympathetic people are so overcome by the grief of another at a funeral that the bereaved is forced to console his supposed comforter.

In contrast, empathy experiences the feelings of another without losing one's own identity. Empathetic people *feel* the hurt of another but are not *disabled* by it.

An empathetic person:

• possesses a sensitive, accurate understanding of the other person's feelings while maintaining a certain separateness from that person.

• can perceive situations that "trigger" others' feelings.

• relates well and communicates with people in such a way that they feel accepted and understood.[2]

At the other end of the sympathy-empathy pendulum, we find apathy. Apathy is defined as a lack of feeling, interest, or concern. Well-known author Edmond Burke said, "All that is necessary for the forces of evil to win the world is for enough good men and women to do nothing."

When I am apathetic, I am *uninvolved*. Excessive detachment from other people and their feelings results in a dwarfed existence.

Often we hear of helping professionals becoming "hardened" by the frequency of dealing with unhealthy and dysfunctional lifestyles. This occupational hazard of police and counselors could easily become yours as you reach out to help those around you.

Which of the following phrases do you find yourself saying most often?

Apathy says, "I don't care."

Empathy says, "Looks like you are feeling really down today."

Sympathy says, "You poor thing."

Apathy says, "That's your problem."

Empathy says, "Sounds as if you were really hurt by that."

Sympathy says, "I feel just dreadful for you."

Suppose a man falls into a well. Mr. Apathy strolls by, gazes down into the well and says, "Boy, aren't you a klutz, falling into that well. You'd better figure a way out."

Mr. Sympathy is out picking forget-me-nots. While reaching for a particularly beautiful blossom, he stumbles onto the well, leans over it and says, "Oh, I feel so sorry for you down in that well." He then proceeds to jump in the well with the man and hands him the flowers. Now we have two helpless people in the well.

Finally Mr. Empathy pulls up in his unmarked rescue truck, pushes unnoticed through the crowd of onlookers, sizes up the depth of the well, and readies the tools necessary to make the rescue. "Hold on," he instructs the victims. "Don't use up your oxygen by talking, and we'll have you out of there within the hour."

Forty-five minutes later, Mr. Empathy grunts one last time as he hoists the men out of the well.

As active listeners, we have the opportunity to make a difference in our world. Because we have walked through much pain, we have learned valuable lessons in life.

As you sit beside a hurting friend listening to her heartbeat, she'll be moved, she'll be comforted. She will hate to see you go.

12

...

Loving Again: "New Normal"

"Amy! Dinner's ready. Come and set the table," I asked our then ten-year-old daughter.

"Later, Mom, later—not now," she balked.

"Amy, I need you to set the table now!" I countered, my voice becoming testy.

"No, Mom, I can't do it now!" she refused belligerently.

We became tense and tight with each other. In the middle of this discussion, Duane appeared. "Amy, you need to set the table for your mother now."

She shrugged her shoulders and went off to do it.

As we sat down at the table a few moments later, Duane announced solemnly, "I think we have some unfinished business to take care of before we eat." He focused on me. "Joanne, I'm really disappointed in what's going on between you and Amy." Then he turned to Amy. "I don't like the way you've been treating your mother." He motioned to a drawer in the kitchen. "Bring me one of our tea towels, Amy, please." Then he instructed me, "Take off your glasses, Joanne."

I didn't know what was going on, but I knew it was better not to argue.

"Amy, roll up the towel like a blindfold and put it over Mom's eyes so that she can't see."

She did and everything went dark. I couldn't see a thing.

"It looks like a trust level has been broken between you," Duane went on. "Let's see what we can do about that."

"Amy, pretend your mother's blind. Let's go for a walk. Joanne, all you have to do is follow Amy's lead."

I stood, took a step, and immediately tripped over my own feet. I was sure Amy would lead me to the nearby basement stairs, give me one big shove and say, "Too bad, you deserve it!"

Amy sensed my reticence. "Mom, are you going to trust me?" she asked gently.

Would I? I had to decide at that moment if I could trust her. After wrestling in my mind, I chose to release the tension, give her my hands, and let her lead me. As I trusted her to take care of me, I did not slip nor trip over my feet again. I began to walk right next to her. We walked effortlessly together.

We walked all around the house. As we returned to the kitchen, she removed the blindfold and we fell into each other's arms. This simple exercise provided the vehicle that restored the broken trust in our relationship.

In the grieving process, we find ourselves walking down an unfamiliar path. We have a choice here. We can try to worm our way out of our predicament, spend sleepless nights counting our fears, or decide to trust.

Trusting God on this unfamiliar path is like walking blindfolded. People ask, "Will I ever be the same? Will I ever be normal again?"

No and yes. You'll never be your "old" normal self again. You will be a different type of normal I call "New Normal." Different doesn't mean bad, but it does involve change. In order to walk down this new path, I have discovered some tools to pave the way.

1. *Explore your strengths and weaknesses.* Take stock of your assets and liabilities, strengths and weaknesses. Suppose one of your strengths is that you're good at building friendships. By nature, I am attracted to people—I simply love people. When I began walking through New Normal, I decided to rekindle the gift of hospitality that lay dormant since Duane's death. As a couple, we had hosted hundreds of get-togethers and even taught hospitality classes for years. Yet, singleness had affected my entire lifestyle.

Since hospitality was an integral part of who I was, I decided I would bravely step out and organize a friendship dinner to bring people together who had recently suffered the loss of a mate. The purpose of this dinner was not for romance but simply to help fill that lonely void. The first dinner was so well-received, I planned one almost every month thereafter. A friend catered the dinners for a nominal charge, and everyone paid their own way. Several strong friendships began out of this "friendship experiment."

One way to develop your strengths is to welcome new relationships. I like to see people as volumes of books in a library. So many people have developed strengths in the areas where I'd like to learn and grow. As I observe their lives, I want to rid myself of intimidation and instead learn from them, explore the price they've paid to be where they are. I have friends who are artistic, medical, mechanical, bookworms, and everything in between. We trade skills and information sometimes, but more importantly, I have enlarged my circle of friends—all ages, all types.

If socializing is not your strong area, reach out and make some contacts by enrolling in community education. Church groups offer all kinds of opportunities for people to get involved.

The time you formerly invested in the person you lost opens up extra time for new activities. Perhaps you could offer aid to a community project or become an adopted grandpa or grandma, aunt or uncle, brother or sister.

Realize you have valuable assets to invest in others' lives. Get serious about improving the quality of your life.

2. *Embrace solitude.* Take the responsibility to find out who you are. Explore your strengths and weaknesses. Prepare to find out all you can about yourself. Develop your skills. If places in your life need molding and changing, be honest with yourself and grow. Learn to be alone with yourself without props—no music, TV, or radio—simply silence. Think of home as a place where you can lock the door behind you, pull the curtain shut and say, "This is my world, and I belong here."

I began to develop a relationship with myself. I spent some concentrated time finding out who I was. You know what? I discovered I liked being with myself all alone.

An integral part of enjoying silence embodies the quality of contentment. Contentment is being content with the content of your life. The Institute in Basic Life Principles defines contentment as "realizing God has provided everything I need for my present happiness."[1]

While alone with myself, I've come to understand me. By thoroughly checking out my strengths and weaknesses, I've recognized and analyzed my fears in certain areas. I admitted them to God. "Help, God! I'm so afraid." As you do this, your trust in God will grow as will your ability to move ahead with your life.

After you have mastered and become comfortable with embracing solitude, befriend some books. I engage in much reading and writing—exploring and getting new understanding. I have learned to be at peace with myself and enjoy the luxury of silence.

When you need company, learn to ask for it. When you need time alone, use it—not as a crutch to escape from your challenges, but to renew and inspire your perspective.

Following are some activities you can do alone:

shopping
browsing in a card shop
gardening
playing an instrument
driving
flower arranging
reading
fishing
sewing
crafts

One man ventured out to a single's club. He entered the room to find four women around a card table playing bridge. They didn't even look up. He left and never went back. You'll need to test some markets to see where you fit in. It's stretching and scary.

I wasn't in New Normal too long before I felt it was time for me to learn how to move into a new situation by myself. When I had the opportunity to go to a resort alone,

I planned a weekend of reading, writing, and thinking. I invited my daughter to drive up and join me for dinner on Friday night.

When Amy arrived, we walked to a lovely restaurant for dinner. We enjoyed an enriching evening talking for several hours at the table. Finally, it was time for Amy to go home.

"Thanks for the wonderful evening, Mom," she said as she hugged me goodbye.

The next night I returned to the same restaurant alone to test my strengths. I brought no props—no books, newspapers, or paperwork. I walked into the restaurant and the maitre d' said, "How many for dinner?"

"One," I said and smiled.

He frowned. "One? Only one for dinner?"

"Yes."

He led me to a section where three separate couples sat at tables. "Sir, if you don't mind, I'd like to sit over here on this other side."

He shrugged his shoulders. "Do whatever you want to do."

I gulped and sat down.

In a few minutes the waiter appeared. "Well, have you decided what you want to eat?" he asked gruffly.

I ordered. I had barely placed my napkin in my lap when he brought the hors d'oeuvres and the salad at the same time. The night before when Amy and I had dined together, we first got the hors d'oeuvres, then the salad with chilled forks, and then much later, the main course.

Here I was alone. The appetizers and the salad came together (no chilled forks), immediately followed by the main course. When I finished the main course, the waiter popped up. "Well, are you ready for dessert?"

"No, thank you, I'd just like some tea."

Very quickly, he returned with my bill. I was testing my strengths to see if I could do this alone. I found out that people didn't want me to be there alone. It's not easy in some places to grow.

3. *Be thankful.* Develop an attitude of gratitude. Express your gratitude and love to those around you.

Make a list of ten items for which you're thankful. Do this every day for a week. Your list may include seemingly insignificant items you may have often overlooked. *Do not duplicate any item.* I did this while taking my nightly bath. For an entire year, I kept a piece of paper next to the tub so I could quickly jot down my thankfulness list. A sample list went like this:

I'm thankful for:
- soap
- wash cloth
- bath towel
- toothpaste
- toothbrush
- hot water
- pillow
- clean sheets
- electricity
- waterbed

This simple activity is not merely busywork. You would be amazed at how much these "little things" mean when loss turns our lives topsy-turvy. Psalm 145:2 says, "Every day [with its new reasons] will I bless You [affectionately and gratefully praise You]; yes, I will praise Your name forever and ever" (TAB).

I made a list of people I wanted to thank. On the top of my list was Duane's cardiologist. I set up the appointment. As I pulled up to the hospital, a wave of memories flooded over me. The last time I was here was the day before Duane died. On that day the doctor had proclaimed Duane in great health and said he would see us in six months.

The nurse ushered me into the doctor's office, and I took a deep breath and sat down. "Doctor, I just want to thank you for being such a great physician. I so appreciate the years of tender and professional care you gave Duane and all the support you gave me. I remember when Duane went through open-heart surgery years ago, and you made yourself available day and night. Thank you for being there. Thank you for giving Duane such hope."

Tears welled up in his eyes. "You came here today to thank me?" he asked incredulously. "I have all Duane's latest X-rays and was sure you were going to want a reason for Duane's death."

"No, sir. I just want to say thanks. Thank you so much for all you did."

Develop an attitude of gratitude. Both you and others will benefit.

4. *Talk about the loss in a normal way.* When you talk about your loved one now, you don't cry as much. You seem to portray an almost emotional detachment from the pain of the experience. You have a new ability to enjoy the memory, without being devastated by it. You can actually smile as you recall the past.

5. *Receive help without feeling like you need to earn it.* You become secure enough in your new role to accept the support your friends want to give you. No strings are attached to their love and no obligations on your part are needed to reciprocate out of duty. You are in a new place and willing to accept a balanced dependence on others, completely free of guilt.

When receiving help, I learned to say simply, "Thank

you very much."

6. *Watch your perspective and priorities change.* You are no longer bound by the role you formerly carried. The priorities associated with being someone's mother, father, wife, husband, or friend has changed. You are free to take on different responsibilities as your perspective modifies your new role.

When I turned fifty, my friends staged a surprise party for me. First, they took me to a rather bizarre restaurant where waiters tie helium balloons to your hair and perform impromptu songs while bantering back and forth with the customers and each other. I was so nervous wondering what was going to happen to me that I could hardly eat. After dinner, a tuxedoed young man walked up to the table and said, "Are you Joanne Smith?"

I hesitated—after all, anything could happen at this place. "Why?" I asked, trying to figure out what was going on.

"Your car is waiting outside," the man declared.

"Is this a joke? What car?"

"Follow me," he instructed politely.

As we stood, the waiters sang a corny love song, harassed me one last time, and we exited. We walked outside under the restaurant canopy where a beautiful stretch limousine was parked with the door opened.

"Hi, Mom. Happy birthday!" greeted my daughter Amy from inside the car.

I climbed inside, followed by my friends. We drove around sipping apple juice in stemmed glasses. Amy was hungry so we drove through McDonald's so she could grab a quick dinner. We passed out of the drive-through, and across the street at a restaurant a large lighted signboard read: "Happy Fiftieth Birthday, Joanne Smith."

We parked at the restaurant entrance. The chauffeur

opened the door and helped me out. Judy guided me down the entry corridor. She slipped over to a glossy white grand piano and began to play as the guests stood and applauded. I'll always remember my emotion as I entered the restaurant and saw such loving friends amid balloons, a giant banner, flowers, and a large display of photographs spanning my life. I hurried from one table to the next, hugging each guest. For this widow, it was one special landmark.

The function of celebrations is to pound a stake in the ground, commemorating the ultimate victory won by those who keep on keeping on. I have walked through many personal rejections, losses, and hard times besides the death of my husband. When it comes time for celebration, I need all those I love dearly to rejoice with me. Support in times of celebration is as important as support during sorrow.

I remember my disappointment when celebrating the premiere of the Grief Release video series. After months of hurdles, the finished product finally arrived. We were ready to celebrate. I sent out special invitations to everyone I thought wouldn't want to miss this occasion— people who were praying for the project, dear friends, and a few key leaders who had shown interest in the project. I usually plan way ahead so people's schedules are free, and I always add, "R.S.V.P." so I can plan seating and refreshments.

I remember several calls from people I was sure would come. After all, I had been there for them, over and over.

"Joanne," one caller remarked, "this is Rosalie. I'd really love to be at your video celebration, but I have a 'Save the Whales' meeting that night. I just can't get out of it."

"Oh, I understand," I responded. But I wasn't sure I

did. That excuse deeply penetrated my heart. I was so disappointed.

After my priorities changed and I discovered how important is was for people to be there for me, I made a special effort to be there for others. Here are some principles I put into practice.

a. *Accept invitations whenever you can and show up on time.* The biggies on my list are weddings, funerals, birthdays, anniversaries, and victory celebrations. Accept them not as a duty, but as an investment in the relationship. Accept them as a thank offering for all the people who walked through your hard time with you.

People have always been important to me. Being there for someone is so paramount that I practically turn somersaults to arrange to attend an important event. I remember the gratitude of one friend when I went to court with her on the day of her final divorce decree. It had nothing to do with the moral issue of divorce and everything to do with friendship and support. Often I have gone with a friend or grief class member to say a final goodbye to their lost relationship. My presence made a difference—not just for them, but for me as well.

When we make an effort to support our friends with our presence, important changes occur. Our friendship is deepened and our love renewed. The Bible says, "He who refreshes others will himself be refreshed" (Prov. 11:25).

b. *Make an effort.* Although it isn't easy, our presence does make a difference. Rearrange schedules. Often we place a higher priority on a dentist appointment than crucial commitments to our friends.

c. *Schedule a makeup date.* If you absolutely can't be there, don't feel guilty. When it's impossible to meet your friend's need, communicate how very sorry you are. Make a date right then for the two of you to get together to share about the event. Don't procrastinate. Demonstrate that your commitment goes beyond mere lip service. Send a note of congratulations or sympathy. State your regrets at not being able to attend.

7. *Learn to love again—verbalize "I love you."* You are free to make new choices about loving. If your friendship died, you can risk making a new one. Even if you shy away from new "loves" because you fear future loss, you can love again. Although your child was the most treasured gift in your life, you can love again. Even if you were burned by a relationship gone awry, you can love again.

A friend wrote a letter to me in which she shared about our similar losses. She affirmed my walk and encouraged me by sharing her experience of God providing her an even deeper relationship in a second husband after the death of her beloved first husband. She said, "Your capacity to love is much greater due to the loss you have suffered. If I had to choose between my late husband and my new husband, it would be the latter." She had learned to love again because she had worked through the loss. God does indeed increase our capacity to love after we embrace our pain and resolve our loss.

C. S. Lewis once said,

> To love at all is to be vulnerable. Love anything, and your heart will certainly be wrung and possibly be broken. If you want to make sure of keeping it intact, you must give your heart to no one, not even to an animal. Wrap it carefully round with hobbies and little luxuries; avoid all entanglements; lock it up safe in the casket or coffin of your selfishness. But in that casket—safe, dark, motionless, airless—it will change. It will not be

broken; it will become unbreakable, impenetrable, irredeemable ... the only place outside Heaven where you can be perfectly safe from all the dangers ... of love is Hell![2]

8. *Gain great compassion for others in pain.* You can no longer walk through life blithely ignoring trauma. Your grief has carved a permanent mark on any apathetic attitudes you once harbored regarding human suffering. Because you have hurt and are being healed, you want to help. Not only do you desire to reach out, your heart is prepared to do so because of the pain you've suffered. Compassion is no longer a merciful inborn trait, but a honed skill at the college of emotional pain. You understand because you have walked through similar pain.

9. *Learn to say no without feeling guilty.* Has the flu bug laid you up for a week or more? When I suffer such a setback, I find that the work piles up. As soon as the tiniest bit of strength surges through my body, I want to bolt out of bed, grab the vacuum cleaner, and make up for lost time. This behavior is the root of the "relapse." When walking through grief, we often tire of being sad and fatigued. At the first sign of returning to normal, many people make the mistake of reverting to a "pre-grief" schedule. If you want to keep regaining emotional and physical strength, I suggest you follow my tips for saying no.

Did you know that saying no is scriptural? Have you found yourself trapped in an impossible schedule by simply being an agreeable "yes" person? Take heed—help is on the way.

Titus 2:11 says, "For the grace of God that brings salvation has appeared to all men. It teaches us to say 'No' to ungodliness and worldly passions, and to live self-controlled, upright and godly lives in this present age."

Ungodliness sometimes disguises itself in perfectly plausible ways. Even those in the body of Christ will force what they think is God's will for you by saying, "I think God would have you accept the committee chairmanship position."

To walk in New Normal, I need to say no to some things outside my home. Twenty-four hours are in each day. Family size, job responsibilities, ages of children, care for older parents or grandparents may vary, but we all have to eat, wear clean clothes, and take care of our homes. All these responsibilities take time. Learning to say no will give us the time we need.

Why Should I Say No?

a. *For productivity.* I need time to myself to be productive. Have you ever found yourself bogged down with so many projects that you can't seem to complete any? Perhaps you flit from one to another, never completing one before you start six more. Saying yes to too many activities restricts productivity by paralyzing our motivation. Say no for productivity.

b. *For creativity.* It's difficult for free-flowing creative ideas to enter a scattered brain. How many beautiful songs are written in the rush between Burger King's drive-up window and an all important board meeting? How many sewing projects are completed on the run?

c. *For accountability.* We only have one body, and we're responsible for it. If we overload our body and stress it needlessly, we pay.

d. *For receptivity.* It takes time to hear from God. Have you ever tried meditating on the run? "Well, God, I overslept and I have all these things going on, and I have three minutes to get your input."

e. *For control.* Who's going to run your life? Don't

allow an eagerness to help your fellow man thrust you into the fast lane going the wrong way. Step on the brakes and pull over. Get control.

Why I Can't Say No

Two reasons prevail why we don't say no. One is our expectations of ourselves. I think I should be able to do this. After all, I have all God's power in me. I should be able to "run and not grow weary." Wait a minute. Did you read the first part of the verse? It says, "Those whose *hope is in the Lord* will renew their strength. They will soar on wings like eagles; they will run and not grow weary, they will walk and not be faint" (Isa. 40:31, italics added). The promise isn't a blank check for those who say yes to every offer and obligation, making unrealistic demands on the human body.

I feel like I must not fail. I feel inadequate. A lot of people have their identities involved in their work. I went through that when I was on staff at a large church once. Then a massive budget cut severed my job, and I felt worthless. I was so totally wrapped up in what I did, and now I no longer did it. My thinking muddled as I tried to figure out who I was. It took me months to get through it. I went through an incredible stripping of attitudes negating my very person. When I finally realized my true worth was in Jesus Christ, I could be at peace. Establish your own identity.

We have this tremendous need for human approval. Our success becomes dependent upon others' opinions. Saying yes becomes a trap to win approval.

Another reason we don't say no rests in others' expectations of us. I can't fail them—I'd feel guilty. In reality, the only time I should feel guilty is when my heart attitude is wrong. People make us feel guilty or hostile—God doesn't. A lot of people say, "I can't fail them—I'm afraid of their hostility," or "I'd feel guilty for letting them down." I am not responsible for the other person's reactions, only for God's purposes in my life. Another excuse is "I'll be rejected." Guess what? Not everybody is going to like you all the time. You will not be loved by everyone. You will feel rejected. Don't let it throw you.

When Should I Say "No"?

a. *When it is clearly inappropriate to my position.* You have a new position now and old responsibilities may or may not fit. Establish whether saying yes fits the new you.

b. *When it is someone else's job.*

c. *When I set up expectations that I know I can't continue.* I may hope I can, but my hopes are totally unrealistic time-wise.

d. *When I have a gut-level feeling I am biting off more than I can chew.*

e. *When I can think of someone who could do it better.* I may be flattered at being asked, but I know someone else who is just right for the job.

f. *When I can think of a better time to do it.* "Thank you for asking me, but I think that if you ask me again next year, I could do it."

g. *When saying yes would threaten something I have already said yes to.*

h. *When I do not have the savings of time and energy.* It's time to move away from looking exhausted all the time.

What to Say No To

a. *Establish a criteria for saying yes.* I can never do this until I understand and establish priorities. What is

144

currently expected of me every day? Write a job description for yourself.

b. *Changing patterns requires a review of commitments.* As family situations change, I need to say no to commitments for which I formerly said yes.

c. *Work out your six-month goals.* A year is too long for me, and I find that even the six-month ones need to be written in sand.

d. *Decide on a certain amount of time for each priority.* If possible, lay out on paper all daily and weekly schedules. Remember to include one hour a day for emergencies.

e. *Review your plan with the Master Planner.* Early every morning I check out my day with the Lord. I ask for specific guidance on how to schedule the day. I ask for help in being open and flexible.

How to Say No

a. *Say no firmly but gently.* Recognize the compliment someone has paid you by asking you to assume a responsible position. Be aware of the other's keen disappointment.

b. *Don't give reasons.* Excuses lead us into quicksand. Let your no simply be no.

c. *Don't put them off.* Procrastination is not the answer. Procrastination is the assassination of motivation. You'll have this nagging, unfinished business hovering over you if you answer with "I'll think about it" when you know the answer is no. If you do need to pray about it, commit to a time to give your decision. Then follow through with an answer.

d. *When you say no, offer an alternative, if possible.* Suggest someone else or another plan.

10. *Begin to think new thoughts.* No longer think of the loss twenty-four hours a day. Allow yourself the freedom to include new people in your life. Develop competence so you can learn to do some things for yourself.

Grief has a way of building up. Months may go by. You'll think you're doing well, and then one day suddenly you start crying and feel the need to talk with someone. This doesn't mean you're slipping. This is part of New Normal.

Learn the balance of dependence and independence. After my father died, I taught my mother how to use the bus system in our city. She goes almost everywhere by herself. When she needs help, she knocks on my door and says, "Jo, will you help me here?" Although she's in her seventies and totally deaf, she's learned how to be independent.

As your focus changes and you're thinking new thoughts, you'll find you need to set goals. To commit to these goals in a positive way, write them down.

Writing down goals helps you organize your thoughts and forces you to plan what you will accomplish in the days to come. A goal is simply a statement of what you want to see accomplished in a certain period of time. For example, you may want to clean out your closets by the end of next month.

Suppose you gave yourself eight weeks. You have eight closets. You know you must clean *one closet a week* to meet your goal. This doesn't sound as overwhelming as saying, "I have eight closets to clean out."

Often in the grieving process your goal will not be task-oriented, but perhaps be an attitude goal you may want to incorporate into your life.

For example, when reaching New Normal, you stand in front of the mirror and proclaim, "This year I'm going to take charge of my life. I'll write in my journal, stay with an exercise program, and take off thirty pounds."

Use the building blocks on the next two pages to help you strengthen your resolve. Make yourself accountable to someone for the next thirty days. Choose and modify at least three building blocks to re-establish your life. I made goals using these blocks and saw my goals come to pass.

Remember that grief is the process of putting back together the pieces of a broken heart—a hole so deep in the middle of your heart that it aches and hurts and you think it will never stop hurting.

In New Normal, visualize your heart-shaped puzzle. You have picked up the pieces of your broken heart and slowly and steadily placed them one by one—until all the pieces of your heart are together. You are now whole. Piece by piece—weeping, writing, talking, saying good-bye to the relationship, releasing your anger, resolving your guilt, and exercising—your heart heals. When you place the last piece into the center of the puzzle you see an inscription. It reads, "Happiness is an inside job."

Building Blocks

Use these building blocks as a guide to help you establish your personal goals.

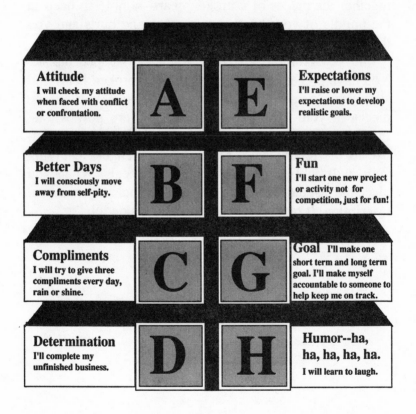

Attitude
I will check my attitude when faced with conflict or confrontation.

A

E

Expectations
I'll raise or lower my expectations to develop realistic goals.

Better Days
I will consciously move away from self-pity.

B

F

Fun
I'll start one new project or activity not for competition, just for fun!

Compliments
I will try to give three compliments every day, rain or shine.

C

G

Goal I'll make one short term and long term goal. I'll make myself accountable to someone to help keep me on track.

Determination
I'll complete my unfinished business.

D

H

Humor--ha, ha, ha, ha, ha.
I will learn to laugh.

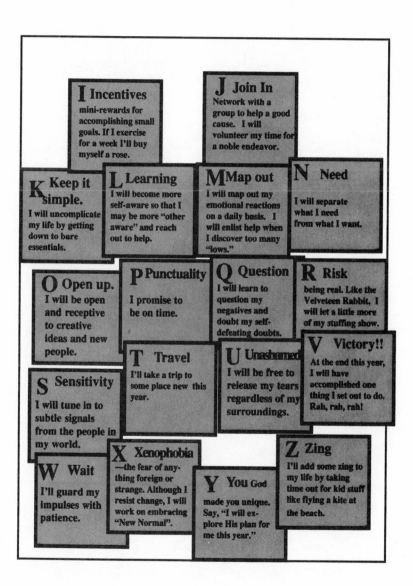

I Incentives
mini-rewards for accomplishing small goals. If I exercise for a week I'll buy myself a rose.

J Join In
Network with a group to help a good cause. I will volunteer my time for a noble endeavor.

K Keep it simple.
I will uncomplicate my life by getting down to bare essentials.

L Learning
I will become more self-aware so that I may be more "other aware" and reach out to help.

M Map out
I will map out my emotional reactions on a daily basis. I will enlist help when I discover too many "lows."

N Need
I will separate what I need from what I want.

O Open up.
I will be open and receptive to creative ideas and new people.

P Punctuality
I promise to be on time.

Q Question
I will learn to question my negatives and doubt my self-defeating doubts.

R Risk
being real. Like the Velveteen Rabbit, I will let a little more of my stuffing show.

S Sensitivity
I will tune in to subtle signals from the people in my world.

T Travel
I'll take a trip to some place new this year.

U Unashamed
I will be free to release my tears regardless of my surroundings.

V Victory!!
At the end this year, I will have accomplished one thing I set out to do. Rah, rah, rah!

W Wait
I'll guard my impulses with patience.

X Xenophobia
—the fear of anything foreign or strange. Although I resist change, I will work on embracing "New Normal".

Y You God
made you unique. Say, "I will explore His plan for me this year."

Z Zing
I'll add some zing to my life by taking time out for kid stuff like flying a kite at the beach.

13

...

Beyond Grief Release: "They Sang Purposefully Ever After . . ."

By the time you have worked through the preceding chapters, you'll have tramped many miles of new roads. You may have stumbled some along the way, kicked a few rocks, or muddied the track under you with tears, but you've come this far. Hooray for you. You've got courage.

I would be remiss if I didn't let you in on a little secret that helped turbo-charge me through the process. At one point during my journey, the Lord had impressed me that my hope would not be cut off (see Prov. 24:14). The Living Bible expresses it like this: "There is hope for you! A bright future lies ahead!"

Many people in the grief process are convinced that their hope has already been cut off. This scripture seems to contradict what they've just walked through. Such a wonderful promise is difficult to believe. However, through all the pain, I've discovered that God is still in the business of fulfilling dreams. I began to believe that I wasn't at a dead-end road. He had some new paths for me to take. I embraced that scripture and began to believe again.

Since I needed something specific to believe in, I decided to set a new goal. I didn't just make it up. I had to discern my desires. What did I want to see happen in my life? Did I want to remarry? Did I want to stay single? It wasn't a flippant notion or decision.

I found that the deep desire in my heart was that I wanted to get married again. I'm not talking about casually whipping off a goal and expecting God to honor it. I spent a lot of time praying about my future and considering all facets of my life. I wrote down the pluses and minuses of singleness and the assets and liabilities of married life. I tried in every way to sort through this list to set my goal for the year. After much prayer, I knew my goal was now to "Meet My Mate in '88."

Shortly thereafter I read this scripture:

"Sing, O barren, you who did not bear; break forth into singing and cry aloud (break out into loud and joyful song). Enlarge your house; build on additions; spread out your home! For you will soon be bursting at the seams! Do not be afraid; you will not suffer shame. Do not fear disgrace; you will not be humiliated!" (Isa. 54: 1, 2, 4 TAB).

Although these verses might seem somewhat irrelevant to you, I decided to listen closer and dig deeper into their meaning for me.

I call it "singing to the barrenness." Now I know what barrenness is in the literal sense since I have never been able to conceive a baby. But the barrenness I'm talking about relates to the empty, vacant, bare, bleak, desolate, unfruitful, void areas of our lives. We all have them regardless of the nature of our loss. Yours may be an emotional, physical, spiritual, or financial need.

My barrenness was in the area of marriage. I had slept in an empty bed for four years when I read this scripture. No matter how silly it might have seemed, I decided to take God at his word and sing. Since the Psalms are filled with prayers set to music, I know this practice is scripturally sound. So I sang. I sang to the Lord about my empty marriage bed. I sang gratefully, untiringly, consistently, tearfully, triumphantly, with lots of faith and with only a glimmer of hope. I sang in the morning, in the evening, and in the middle of the night. I sang when I felt like it, and I sang when I could barely get out the words.

Since our hope will not be cut off, what do we do when the disappointments and challenges hit us? One night I was about to start a new grief class. I'd received several cancellation phone calls, and I was afraid that no one would attend. So I sang, "Lord, I sing to the fear that nobody's going to show up for class tonight. I know that your perfect love casts out fear, and I ask you to fill me with peace." Immediately, that awful gnawing and unsettledness disappeared, and I felt real peace.

I not only sang in private, but I taught it publicly. I demonstrated it wherever I traveled to speak. I had a lot of fun teaching in this area. Although I hadn't seen the answer yet, I taught it. Even when I was scheduled to teach on other subjects, it ultimately came up as an alternate method of prayer.

As I taught classes, spoke in churches and business groups, moderated radio programs and traveled, I kept singing to the barrenness in my bed. When I was all alone and uncertain about my future, I chose to sing instead of letting the enemy defeat me.

I sang to God in all areas of my barrenness—health problems, relationship challenges, and financial problems. I simply opened my mouth and used any combination of tones or an old familiar tune. I sang, "God, I'm barren in energy. I ask you to give me fruitfulness in this area. I praise you, Lord, for I know you are faithful to give me strength and vitality."

As I sang, I refused to give up hope. When I needed help, I called Judy and we sang together over the phone. When I was in public, I sang in my head—that's called singing with your mind. First Corinthians 14:15 says, "So what shall I do? I will pray with my spirit, but I will also pray with my mind; I will sing with my spirit, but I will also sing with my mind."

Recently I was called to the hospital room of a woman who had attempted suicide. She had taken twelve bottles of pills following her birthday party. As I sat, watching the horrible stomach pumping ordeal, I sang to her emotional and physical barrenness. I prayed for her in song—silently in my head. I believe I was placed in that very spot to be there for her, and she'll never know it.

As I sang, I was spurred on by remembering the faith of Paul and Silas in prison. "But about midnight, as Paul and Silas were praying and singing hymns of praise to God, and the [other] prisoners were listening to them, suddenly there was a great earthquake, *so that the very foundations of the prison were shaken; and at once all the doors were opened and everyone's shackles were unfastened*" (Acts 16:25, 26 TAB, italics added).

Although I felt as helpless as a prisoner when it came to believing God would send this forty-eight-year old widow a husband, I was intrigued with the power of Paul and Silas' song. It caused an earthquake that shook the whole prison and freed everyone there.

And so, I intensified my song to God about the barren-ness in my life. I taught people in my classes to sing. I don't mean la-dee-dah professional singing, but rather "wholehearted" singing. The kind you do in the shower when nobody's around. Or the wails you cry out when you think no one but God is listening.

Some areas of my life were so barren I sang until I had peace. I began singing in January about a potential mate, and nothing happened. I sang by faith for many months. Finally, nine months later, I met Irv.

In September 1988, I traveled to British Columbia to speak about grief at a conference. Judy and her husband Steve and I drove to Vancouver, B.C., stayed overnight at a hotel, and boarded the camp ship to Malibu the next day. We arrived early because the trip took around eight hours and good seats were scarce. While Steve parked the car, Judy hauled in the luggage, and I ran ahead to land us some seats. I secured a booth in the dining room.

Shortly, a lovely blond woman approached me. "Do you have room for a family at your table?" she inquired.

"Well, how big is your family?" I asked, sizing up the seating space.

"Five of us, including two children," she answered.

"Sure. I think there's room."

She went back to find her brood while I spread our coats across the seats. When she returned, she smiled and introduced everyone. "I guess if we're spending eight hours together we should get to know each other. I'm Mardi Newman and this is my husband, Jeff. This is my father, Irv Bloom. This is Holly, our daughter and her friend, Jennifer. Jeff will be the camp doctor this weekend."

When Steve and Judy showed up, we made introductions again.

Mardi asked me, "What do you do?"

"I'm a grief counselor. I'm speaking this weekend on the subject of loss."

"Oh," she seemed intrigued. Most people aren't too thrilled with the subject of grief—until someone dies or leaves them.

Among my teaching materials, we found a full-page story published by a Portland newspaper. I was featured on the cover in living color, holding a large cuddly "grief" teddy bear. Judy handed the paper to Mardi. She read the article and passed it to Irv. "This is really something," she commented. "I'm sure you've helped a lot of people."

"Well, it is rewarding. So many hurting people are out there."

"What do you do, Irv?" I asked, changing the subject.

"Well, I'm semi-retired as a graphic designer. Currently, I work as a massage therapist." His hazel eyes lit up. I couldn't help noticing how his silver hair framed his handsome face.

Judy kicked me under the table and whispered, "Ask him if he's married." (Judy was forever scoping out available men for me—from Korea to Hawaii to Cucamonga.)

The ensuing conversation revealed that Irv's wife died years prior. Judy took an instant liking to Irv. Before long, our table of eight had shrunk to two, and for much of the trip, Irv and I got to know each other.

We docked at the camp, amid a floating brass band and cheering throng. Since this weekend was an adult weekend and composed mainly of couples, Irv and I automatically teamed up. In one group activity we were instructed to join hands. Irv's hands were so strong. When the activity ended, he didn't let go. I looked up into his electric eyes and melted.

When the conference ended, we all exchanged phone

numbers and vowed to meet within the next couple of months.

In November, Judy and I planned to attend a conference in southern California. We booked our flight out of Seattle and scheduled a Newman-Bloom weekend prior to the conference. Steve drove us up to Seattle where we all lodged at the Newman's. We laughed and ate and had a great time playing pickleball on Jeff and Mardi's home sports court. As far as any romantic feelings were concerned, Irv was quite non-committal. I left for California discouraged and depressed. It was nearly the end of 1988, and my hope was waning.

The end of December 1988 arrived, and I kept singing. God had answered so many prayers in other barren areas, but I still hadn't seen an answer to my marriage prayer. I decided to forge ahead with a new motto, "Romance Divine in '89." I would turn fifty this year—half a century. Surely, God had something in store for me during this celebration year.

I received letters and phone calls from all the people whose prayers were answered as they sang through their barren areas in 1988. People continually approached me saying, "Well, did you meet your mate in '88?"

"I don't think so. But my new motto is 'Romance Divine in '89,' " I answered cheerfully.

On New Year's Eve day I received this message on my answering machine: "Hello, Joanne dear. I sure have enjoyed getting to know you this last year. I think our friendship is progressing nicely. I look forward to spending more time with you in '89. Happy New Year!"

I laughed. Four months and three dates later didn't seem like progress to this race horse.

My fiftieth birthday party provided the catalyst to motivating Irv's romantic responses. Judy asked him to make a banner for my surprise party so he was obligated to show up. After the party, Steve and Judy drove Irv and me to my home. Irv was spending the night at Judy and Steve's, but he wanted to share some time alone with me. I built a fire in the basement fireplace. We began to read all the birthday cards. I was so overwhelmed with the generosity of my friends. My gratitude overflowed. In the spontaneity of the moment, we kissed. I can't begin to describe the electricity that surged through me. I was sunk.

The letters and phone calls continued at a snail's pace. I left in May for Korea and Hawaii for two weeks. As I watched all the couples and heard the romantic Hawaiian music, I died inside. I decided I wouldn't come back to Hawaii single.

I was no sooner home when it was time to leave on a ministry trip to Africa. This time I would be gone for three weeks. Three long weeks. I had looked forward to this trip for almost a year, but my heart was torn, half of me wanting to be with Irv.

Shortly after I arrived home from Kenya, on Thursday, July 20th at 10:19 a.m., the phone rang. The voice on the other end of the line said, "Joanne, would you become my beloved wife?"

I cried for ten minutes. "Yes," I managed when I could gain enough composure to speak.

Several weeks later, Irv planted my engagement ring as the "prize" in a Cracker Jacks box. "Joanne, you're my prize. I love you."

I was emotionally ready for marriage. I had already put so much time and effort into thinking it through that I didn't have any fear of marriage. I wasn't flying by the seat of my pants. After I embraced the scripture about singing to and in the barrenness, I implemented the discipline of singing regularly and wholeheartedly.

Early in our friendship Irv and I began to sing to Jesus. Singing has been very special in our relationship. To seal our marriage vows, we chose to sing a love song. "I love you more than anyone, I love you, and I give my heart to you."

"Sing, sing, sing to the barrenness—all day long.

Sing, sing, bring all your troubles, express them in song.

Sing, sing, whate'er betide you, sing through the Spirit of God that's inside you,

Sing continually.

Sing, sing, sing to the barrenness, sing, sing, sing!"

Source Notes

CHAPTER 1

1. Erich Lindemann, "Symptomatology and Management of Acute Grief," *American Journal of Psychiatry*, 101 (1944), p. 148.
2. Dr. James J. Lynch, *The Broken Heart—The Medical Consequences of Loneliness*, (New York: Basic Books, Inc., 1977), p. 56.
3. Dr. Glen W. Davidson, *Understanding Mourning—A Guide for Those Who Grieve,* (Minneapolis: Augsburg, 1984), p. 24.
4. Davidson, p. 24.
5. Sally Squires, "Stress, Separation and Sickness," *Ladies Home Journal,* (March 1989), p. 96.
6. Davidson, pp. 22, 23.

CHAPTER 2

1. Reprinted by permission of Running Press, 125 South 22nd Street, Philadelphia, PA 19103. From *The Velveteen Rabbit*. Copyright 1981 by Running Press. Available from the publisher for $3.95 plus one dollar postage/handling (in paperback).
2. Dr. Larry Crabb, *Inside Out* (Colorado Springs: Nav-Press, 1988), p. 34.
3. Thomas B. Holmes and Richard Rahe, "Stress Rating Scale," *Journal of Psychosomatic Research,* 2 (1967), p. 216.
4. David Gelman with Mary Hager, "Body and Soul," *Newsweek,* (November 7, 1989), p. 88.
5. "Body and Soul," p. 89.

CHAPTER 3

1. Diane Cole, "Grief Lessons: His and Hers," *Psychology Today,* (December 1988), pp. 60, 61.
2. "Grief Lessons: His and Hers," pp. 60, 61.
3. "Grief Lessons: His and Hers," pp. 60, 61.
4. "Grief Lessons: His and Hers," pp. 60, 61.

CHAPTER 4

1. Drs. Carol and Jeff Rubin, "Tis the Season to Be Fighting," *Psychology Today,* (December 1988), pp. 36-39.
2. "Tis the Season to be Fighting," pp. 36-39.

CHAPTER 5

1. Dr. William H. Frey II with Muriel Langseth, *Crying: The Mystery of Tears,* (Minneapolis: Winston Press 1985), p. 12.

2. Greg Levoy, "Tears that Speak," *Psychology Today*, (August 1988), p. 8.
3. "Tears that Speak," p. 10.
4. "Tears that Speak," p. 10.
5. "Tears that Speak," p. 10.
6. "Tears that Speak," p. 10.

CHAPTER 6

1. Joanetta Hendel, "Write Away," *Bereavement Magazine*, (February 1989), pp. 40, 41.
2. "Write Away," pp. 40, 41.

CHAPTER 7

1. Ken Durham, *Speaking from the Heart* (Ft. Worth, TX: Sweet Publishing Co. Inc., 1986), pp. 121, 122.

CHAPTER 10

1. Dave Ross, *A Book of Hugs* (New York: Crowell, 1980).
2. Dave Ross, *More Hugs* (New York: Crowell, 1984).

CHAPTER 11

1. Joseph Bayly, *The View from a Hearse* (Elgin, IL: David C. Cook Publishing Co., 1973).
2. Robert Bolton, *People Skills* (New York: Simon & Schuster, 1979), p. 272.

CHAPTER 12

1. Institute in Basic Life Principles, Oak Brook, IL.
2. C.S. Lewis, *The Four Loves* (Harcourt, Brace & Jovanovich, Inc., Orlando, FL), 1960, p. 157.

Inquiries regarding speaking availability and other correspondence may be directed to Joanne Smith and Judy Biggs at the following address:

> One To Another Ministries
> 4645 SE 33rd Avenue
> Portland, OR 97202
>
> (503) 771-4341